The Market Structure Crisis

Electronic Stock Markets, High Frequency Trading, and Dark Pools

Haim Bodek
Stanislav Dolgopolov

Decimus Capital Markets, LLC

http://www.haimbodek.com
https://decimuscapitalmarkets.com

Copyright © 2015 by Decimus Capital Markets, LLC. *All rights reserved,* including the right of reproduction in whole or in part in any form.

E-published in the United States. November 2015.
Published in the United States. November 2015

ISBN-13: 978-1519279095
ISBN-10: 1519279094

Contact information:

Haim Bodek – Managing Principal

Decimus Capital Markets, LLC
203-359-2625
haim@haimbodek.com

http://haimbodek.com
https://decimuscapitalmarkets.com
Twitter: @HaimBodek

IMPORTANT INFORMATION

This document is intended to serve as general information. The information in this document reflects the views of Decimus Capital Markets, LLC ("DCM") based on prevailing conditions at the time of the publication. The information in this document is subject to change without notice, and DCM assumes no duty to update any information. DCM's opinions, interpretations, and estimates with regards to technological, financial, regulatory, and other areas of expertise, including but not limited to information provided by third parties, constitute DCM's judgment and should be regarded as indicative, preliminary, and for illustrative purposes only. In preparing this document, DCM has relied upon and assumed, without independent verification, the accuracy and completeness of certain information from public sources or provided by third parties. DCM's analysis is not and does not purport to constitute appraisals or forward-looking statements with regards to any assets, securities, or business of other entities.

Nothing in this document should be construed as investment, valuation, appraisal, accounting, regulatory, legal, or tax advice. Furthermore, nothing in this document constitutes a recommendation, solicitation, offer, or commitment to purchase, sell, or underwrite any securities from you, to you, or on your behalf or to extend any credit, provide any insurance product, or enter into any other transaction. Unless otherwise agreed in writing, DCM is not acting as your agent, adviser, or fiduciary. Before you enter into any transaction, you should ensure that you fully understand potential risks and rewards of that transaction, and you should engage and consult with your advisers, as you deem necessary to assist you in making these determinations, including but not limited to your investment advisors, valuation / appraisal experts, accountants, legal, regulatory and / or tax experts.

DCM SHALL NOT BE LIABLE FOR ANY DIRECT, INDIRECT, INCIDENTAL, SPECIAL, CONSEQUENTIAL, OR EXEMPLARY DAMAGES, INCLUDING BUT NOT LIMITED TO DAMAGES FOR LESS OF PROFITS, INCURRED BY YOU OR ANY THIRD PARTY THAT MAY ARISE FROM ANY RELIANCE ON THIS DOCUMENT OR FOR THE RELIABILITY, ACCURACY, OR COMPLETENESS THEREOF.

Table of Contents

I. 20 Predictions for the Future of the Market Structure Crisis 1
II. Reigniting the Order Type Debate 9
III. Deconstructing Maker-Taker 18
    A. *A Gordian Knot for Market Structure?* 18
    B. *Time to Cut the Knot?* 21
IV. The Problem of Fragmentation and Potential Solutions 27
    A. *Fragmentation as a Debated Issue and a Key Driver of HFT* 27
    B. *The Phenomenon of Latency Arbitrage* 29
    C. *The Existence of a Wide Range of Trading Venues* 30
    D. *Different Allocation Mechanisms* 33
    E. *Segmentation* 34
    F. *Regulatory Controls on Fragmentation* 36
    G. *Attacks on Dark Liquidity and the Trade-At Rule* 38
    H. *Impact on Trading Venues and Other Constituencies* 42
V. HFT Regulation and Market Structure Reform 43
    A. *Assessing "Sand in the Wheels" Approaches* 44
    B. *Anti-Disruptive Regulation* 50
    C. *Other Structural Restrictions* 51
    D. *"Plumbing" and the Order Type Controversy* 54
    E. *Outlook for Traders and Other Constituencies* 61
VI. Leveling the Playing Field: Lit and Dark Trading Venues 62
    A. *Recent Enforcement Developments* 62
    B. *Regulatory Immunity* 64
    C. *Fraudulent Conduct* 66
    D. *Ability to Offer Premium Products* 66
    E. *Rise of Innovative / Anti-Gaming / Investor-Oriented Trading Venues* 67
    F. *Dark Pools* 68
    G. *Trading Venues for Other Asset Classes and Diversification Strategies* 71

 H. Assessing the Outlook for Trading Venues 72
VII. Protecting Customers and Achieving Best Execution: Issues for Retail and Institutional Brokers 75
 A. The Duty of Best Execution 76
 B. Joint Review of Allocation Mechanisms 77
 C. Maker-Taker and Order Flow Arrangements 78
 D. Use of Special Order Types 81
 E. Choosing a Proper Execution Channel 82
 F. Discriminatory Treatment 83
 G. Off-Exchange Market Makers 84
 H. Electronic Trading Risk Controls 86
VIII. Litigation and the Impact of Enforcement: The Market Structure Perspective 88
 A. Securities Fraud and New (and Older Analogous) Practices 89
 B. "Front-Running," "Stepping Ahead," and "Order Anticipation" 91
 C. Major Trends in Enforcement as a Guide for Litigation 94
 D. Litigation Landscape 95
 E. Lessons from the City of Providence Class Action Lawsuit .98
IX. Public Comment Letter on Several Order Type-Related Modifications Proposed by the New York Stock Exchange 105
X. The Flash Boys Lawsuit: The End of the Beginning? 120
Appendix A: Summary of Key Enforcement Actions and Lawsuits 128
Appendix B: Selected Market Structure-Related References 136
Available: A Comprehensive Proprietary Research Report on the Market Structure Crisis 140
Available: Haim Bodek's *Problem of HFT* 142
About Decimus Capital Markets, LLC and Its Offerings 145

I. 20 Predictions for the Future of the Market Structure Crisis

Haim Bodek and Stanislav Dolgopolov
Decimus Capital Markets, LLC
August 2015
Originally appeared online in *Tabb Forum*

By the end of 2014, scarcely a day had passed without news on regulatory, legal, and commercial developments relating to the U.S. securities industry's market structure. This unprecedented state of affairs still persists as of mid-2015, albeit with less sensationalism. A truly national debate has been galvanized around the once obscure topic of market structure. As a result, the regulatory framework governing the architecture of securities markets is changing, and our industry should expect the electronic marketplace to go through even more transformations.

Despite the flurry of regulatory changes seeking to enhance stability in securities markets with sophisticated modifications – such as the tick size pilot, volatility bands, the ban of stub quotes, the consolidated audit trail initiative, and several new rules on compliance and integrity – it is prudent to anticipate additional and perhaps even more radical changes to emerge from the intense regulatory, legal, and commercial pressures that weigh on our industry.

The regulatory framework governing securities markets will mutate as a result of the continuing collective pressure on various market structure-related problems by the U.S. Congress, the U.S. Securities and Exchange Commission, and other federal and state regulatory agencies, as well as numerous far-reaching lawsuits filed on behalf of investors. In our opinion, the SEC's leadership has played a very active role in emphasizing the problem of market structure as a top priority and putting forward balanced policy-making goals, while proceeding with landmark enforcement actions against trading venues and other major industry players.

While the "rigged market" paradigm is not especially helpful and perhaps unfortunate, it is certainly true that the current market structure has nurtured a number of systematic and, in many cases, non-transparent asymmetries that may be seen as unfair or inefficient. In our assessment, the current crisis, while being a multifaceted phenomenon, represents a natural reaction to the cumulative effect of these asymmetries, which include preferential market access, superior pricing structures, captive order flow arrangements, and complex order types. Even more so, some of these asymmetries are outright illegal, such as false and misleading statements about certain functionalities provided by trading venues or the very nature of their business models, as exemplified by the "agency only" claims by ITG while its infamous Project Omega was operational. Overall, these asymmetries have been building up for quite a while, often originating in symbiotic relationships, sometimes reinforced by ownership stakes, of these market participants with trading venues.

Another key factor behind the current market structure crisis is regulatory arbitrage, the term that reflects the existence of discrepancies in different regulatory treatments and an unavoidable temptation to "game" them, as well as the exploitation of gray areas in regulation or its unintended implications more generally. Regulatory arbitrage may be a particularly dangerous phenomenon when combined with technological means to make it scalable. Notable examples of regulatory arbitrage in the current environment include the phenomenon of "latency arbitrage," including the exploitation of the "one second exception" of Rule 611 of Regulation NMS, and the usage of "intermarket sweep orders"[1] in

---

[1] *See* Haim Bodek, *Why HFTs Have an Advantage, Part 3: Intermarket Sweep Orders*, TABB FORUM (Oct. 29, 2012), http://tabbforum.com/opinions/why-hfts-have-an-advantage-part-3-intermarket-sweep-orders (registration required).

scenarios outside of the scope originally anticipated by the regulators.

As a conservative prediction, the cumulative impact of regulatory changes is unlikely to result in a truly radical restructuring of the securities industry, although potential changes are likely to address, with varying degrees of intensity, such important areas as latency arbitrage, dark pool transparency, order routing practices in connection with the duty of best execution, internalization practices, market makers' obligations and privileges, market access and electronic trading risks, audit trails, trading systems' operational risks, and cybersecurity. Rest assured, many areas bearing the brunt of regulatory focus and criticism, including the very phenomenon of HFT, will continue to be important facets of securities markets and survive the scenario of aggressive reform.

When we first started tracking the trajectory of the market structure crisis in mid-2014, we did not anticipate that telltale signs of a moderate and sensible approach by the regulators would in fact materialize into a coherent strategy of policy-making and enforcement only a year later. For one thing, the SEC deserves a lot of credit for handling complex issues and zeroing in on specific wrongful practices, as illustrated by the settlements with Direct Edge, UBS, and ITG.[2] The message is clear to an industry that (arguably) has grown accustomed to extracting edge through sophisticated asymmetries and crossing the blurry (and occasionally clear) lines of regulation. It is no longer business as usual. Notwithstanding waves of criticism from the left and the right, the regulators appear to be on top of things in an imperfect world.

Our current forecasts for the market structure crisis and countervailing forces follow below. These forecasts are a mix of

---

[2] *See* ITG Inc. Securities Act Release No. 9887, Exchange Act Release No. 75,672 (Aug. 12, 2015), http://www.sec.gov/litigation/admin/2015/33-9887.pdf; UBS Sec. LLC, Securities Act Release No. 9697, Exchange Act Release No. 74,060 (Jan. 15, 2015), http://www.sec.gov/litigation/admin/2015/33-9697.pdf; EDGA Exch. Inc., Exchange Act Release No. 74,032 (Jan. 12, 2015), http://www.sec.gov/litigation/admin/2015/34-74032.pdf.

anticipated policy reforms, enforcement actions and private lawsuits, and business model changes:

1. The regulators are likely to further address market confidence with targeted enforcement actions that have symbolic meaning and emphasize to-the-letter compliance with the existing laws and regulations.

2. The regulators will proceed with modest changes to the regulatory framework, including additional disclosure requirements and measures to address complexity-related issues, and these changes are likely to rely on pilot studies. Furthermore, some regulatory changes will be implemented by trading venues themselves as a result of the securities industry's cleanup efforts and pressure applied by the regulators.

3. The key components of the regulators' enforcement agenda, which also will spill over to policy-making, as well as private lawsuits, include Regulation NMS, data feeds, order handling, order routing and payment for order flow arrangements, spoofing/layering and other forms of market manipulation, market access, and trading risk/systems controls.

4. Direct congressional intervention into the market structure crisis is unlikely but still possible. Another factor that may lead to significant policy changes is represented by possible judicial re-interpretations of the federal securities statutes.

5. Intervention on the state level (e.g., the State of New York) is a wildcard, with various scenarios of either turf wars or collaboration with the federal regulators, as illustrated by the Barclays lawsuit. A broadly worded state statute, such as New York's Martin Act, can always be used as a threat.

6. The *City of Providence v. BATS* class action lawsuit, despite its gray areas and related setbacks for private lawsuits brought against securities exchanges, has the potential to expose trading venues to significant liability or at least lead to additional enforcement actions and policy reform. Additional mutations of this controversy,

including more-focused lawsuits and new allegations, are already taking place, with even more expected. Other potential defendants are HFTs, integrated securities firms, brokerage firms, and other trading venues.

7. The intense competition and greater transparency within the low-latency space will continue to result in lower margins and thus increase firms' dependency on order flow relationships. This trend will be reinforced by the increasing number of restraints, such as limitations on the usage of data feeds and scrutiny of consolidated-to-private data feed arbitrage. Overall, speed-, plumbing-, and fragmentation-related advantages of HFTs will continue to diminish.

8. The compression in the low-latency trading space will have a knock-down effect on low-latency providers, further erode clearing and execution margins, and divert more activity to new business models (e.g., IEX, execution algos and off-exchange relationships).

9. Major retail and institutional brokers will be subject to intense public and regulatory scrutiny, including lawsuits, on conflicts of interest and the required level of care (e.g., maker-taker, payment for order flow, affiliated dark pools, and complex order types). Private lawsuits will be more aggressive and thus test the legal boundaries of many industry practices.

10. The changing regulatory landscape, including fragmentation-related initiatives, will impose more constraints on different types of trading venues. Dark pool sponsors will likely succumb to pressure to make their trading venues more transparent in terms of their rules/standards and improve value proposition of their products for both institutional and retail investors. Overall, there will be more consolidation and failures, as well as explosive lawsuits, in the trading venue space.

11. Latency arbitrage and various market structure shortcuts/plumbing exploits practiced by HFTs and trading venues will be addressed through regulatory action, including selective enforcement, and private lawsuits.

12. The tick size pilot, including its trade-at feature, should be watched closely as a measure that has a good chance to be adopted on a permanent basis. On the other hand, reforming the tick size regime might not result in anything meaningful, unless internalization, payment for order flow practices, and maker-taker-related issues are adequately addressed. Furthermore, the actual results of this pilot will depend on its specific features and exceptions, which may generate data noise.

13. The regulators will take some steps to address the issue of fragmentation, although aiming at a true synchronization of competing trading venues is unlikely. There is a good chance that some version of the trade-at rule or its functional equivalent ultimately will be retained as one of the easier fixes, resulting in an adverse impact on dark pools and off-exchange market makers.

14. Regulation NMS will be revisited and perhaps even reformed, including the trade-through rule, the ban on locked and crossed markets, and the ban on subpenny pricing, as a result of a comprehensive market structure review by the SEC, including the role played by the Equity Market Structure Advisory Committee. Another scenario is that certain implications of Regulation NMS will be supplanted via other regulatory changes, such as the trade-at rule or more narrow exceptions.

15. The cumulative effect of changes in the registered market-making segment of the securities industry will be significant, and this segment will experience a (modest) revival. However, off-exchange market makers may lose some of their advantages, such as the ability to offer de minimis price improvement or benefits derived from exclusive captive order flow arrangements.

16. The maker-taker pricing model and payment for order flow practices will be scrutinized and probably adjusted by the SEC acting jointly with the securities industry. An outright ban of either mechanism is not very likely, but tighter boundaries and indirect restrictions are possible, especially with regard to implementing a sizable (perhaps even a threefold) reduction in the access fee cap,

addressing conflicts of interest in order routing practices, and ensuring compliance with the duty of best execution.

17. The order type controversy will be partially resolved as a result of combined pressures from several directions, including the securities industry's cleanup efforts, enforcement actions, and private litigation; but the complexity of order types menus will not disappear. Navigating complex order types will remain a challenge for several interested groups, such as institutional investors and their brokers.

18. There will be additional enforcements actions and lawsuits dealing with modern manifestations of market manipulation, such as spoofing/layering. The initial focus will be on bad actors, with many of them operating from overseas, but the regulators will also be addressing brokers' failures to institute proper monitoring and controls.

19. The regulators will be taking a proactive stance on market access, risk controls, and systems controls based on the recently adopted Market Access Rule and Regulation SCI. Infrastructure governance and procedures-related costs will rise and possibly keep escalating with new glitches.

20. The fallout in the dark pool space from Barclays and ITG, as well as other publicized incidents, will involve long-term policy reform in addition to enforcement actions and private lawsuits. The buy-side in particular will raise its standard of due diligence, lower its tolerance for potential legal liability, and rely more extensively on third-party independent expertise as a check on execution quality.

Ultimately, the impact of the market structure crisis becomes a risk management issue for every firm heavily engaged in the U.S. securities industry. It is prudent for any stakeholder to assess trading venues, brokers, service providers, partners, counterparties, and investments in terms of their overall exposure to these regulatory, legal, and commercial pressures. Likewise, one needs to proactively address risks by creating contingency plans to mitigate the damage of interaction with bad or negligent actors and employing analytical services such as TCA.

For firms within the eye of the hurricane, such as trading venues, proprietary traders, and broker-dealers providing execution services, we expect to see additional casualties and perhaps a few more firms extracting tangible benefits from the changes we anticipate. While human capital, financial capital, computing power, and infrastructure can be redeployed, the adjustment process is bound to be very painful for many players that are sensitive or even hypersensitive to a number of factors. Certain business models or trading strategies are exposed to substantial risks, and there are already several casualties of the market structure crisis, such as the CBOE Stock Exchange and LavaFlow ECN, as well as few beneficiaries, most notably, IEX.

II. Reigniting the Order Type Debate

Haim Bodek
Decimus Capital Markets, LLC
August 2014
Originally appeared online in *Tabb Forum*

In her seminal speech – titled "Enhancing Our Equity Market Structure"[1] – Mary Jo White, Chairwoman of the U.S. Securities and Exchange Commission, emphasized that "the large number of complex order types offered by the exchanges ... have been a recent focus of the SEC's examination program." She also asked "the exchanges to conduct a comprehensive review of their order types and how they operate in practice."

This request generated a quick response, but it effectively reinforced an earlier trend in the securities industry. For those following the market structure crisis, the message for the exchanges seemed to be: *This is your chance to come clean.*

The influx of rule filings with regard to advanced order types by securities exchanges, many of them claiming to promote the twin goals of clarification and simplification, comes as no surprise. Witness the lengthy documents on "clarifications" of order types and modifiers submitted by NYSE Arca and Direct Edge, or the simultaneous rule submission by every single equity exchange on the usage of price feeds, including the impact on order handling. Even alternative trading systems, which count among themselves "dark pools," have become more open to releasing their rules despite the lack of a formal regulatory requirement to do so.

---

[1] Mary Jo White, Chairman, U.S. Sec. & Exch. Comm'n, Enhancing Our Equity Market Structure: Remarks at Sandler O'Neill & Partners, L.P. Global Exchange and Brokerage Conference (June 5, 2014), http://www.sec.gov/News/Speech/Detail/Speech/1370542004312#.U99FBGN5WEc.

While many of these filings and other disclosures are likely driven by increased regulatory scrutiny and a desire to appear compliant, the overall goal of removing informational asymmetries is commendable. On the other hand, confusion still persists, and the spate of filings offers minimal disclosure on the order type interactions most central to the order handling asymmetries I have heavily criticized for the past three years. For example, exchanges still have yet to provide full disclosure on order matching engine features and order type interaction that determine queue priority and maker-taker fee allocation, particularly with regard to order handling of advanced forms of Intermarket Sweep Orders (ISOs).

The market structure debate exists in its current format largely because no well-defined framework exists for analyzing and comparing the multitude of trading venue rules with respect to how special order types typically used by high-frequency traders interact with order types used by other classes of traders. While one can imagine a world of excessive disclosure, we have not reached it. Indeed, more disclosure is needed, as well as an appropriate framework for analyzing the pipeline of rule filings.

When I first blew the whistle on order type abuses in my early conversations with Scott Patterson of the *Wall Street Journal* back in 2011, and then with federal and state regulators in greater detail, I focused on several questionable order handling practices. These practices were used by (and/or demanded by) certain HFTs that exploited them with the help of the exchanges and to the obvious and substantial detriment of the public investor. These toxic features had specifically harmed my firm. Moreover, these features, as I argued and continue to argue, have not been adequately disclosed.

The thrust of my complaint has been the problematic interaction between order types designed to accommodate HFT strategies and order types typically employed by the public investor and most agency brokers. These arguments helped give birth to the so-called order type controversy, a term that directly addresses trading venues' obligations to disclose special order type features and order matching engine practices that are typically exploited by HFTs to get an edge over the rest of the electronic crowd. In addition to an

SEC investigation, which appears ongoing, the order type controversy resulted in market structure changes implemented by trading venues starting perhaps as early as late 2011. More recently, this controversy has become a key topic in the raging market structure debate, a central theme in the discussion of unintended consequences of Regulation NMS, and a source of legal claims in class action lawsuits now engulfing a big chunk of the securities industry.

As part of my continued interest in making public these abuses and their means of operation to the detriment of most investors, I summarize below the core claims that have been the focus of my whistleblowing contribution to this debate for the past several years. These original claims provide a framework for answering the critical question: *What is meant by "undocumented" order type features and order matching engine practices?*

Exchange documentation has been materially deficient in several respects, including the following unexplained and undisclosed but significantly harmful features:

> *a. precedence rules that advantage HFT order types over others (including conditions where price-time priority corruption occurs, and conditions where certain order type priority is firm, though other order types are "re-posted" with new booking times);*
>
> *b. rules for "hiding" and "lighting" (including conditions for maintaining a hidden state and triggers for lighting, and conditions where incoming orders have preference over "hidden" states or are subordinate to such "hidden" states, including but not limited to, the impact of DAY ISOs as "lighting" events);*
>
> *c. conditions for adherence to the SIP including the cases where an exchange will use direct feeds in conjunction with the SIP to determine "locking" and "lighting" conditions;*

d. conditions and mechanisms where information about an exchange's protected quotation state management, which normally would be expected to remain local to the exchange order matching engine, is communicated to HFTs in an advantageous manner (i.e., mechanisms in which price sliding reject messages provide "re-posting" guidance for HFTs);

e. conditions of eligibility for maker/taker fees and rebates and conditions where fee transference occurs (including the conditions where non-marketable orders are re-posted to execute against special orders to incur taker fees); and

f. the scenarios where the various price-sliding conditions are applied (with detail provided for both HFT order types and the common public customer order types), as well as full detail on conditions where "Post Only" orders in a hidden state may internally lock a market or otherwise gain precedence over other orders (including such properties as would apply to "Post Only" mid-point orders).

I urge you to do what I have done, and begin a comprehensive assessment of several recent filings using the framework above to determine the extent to which they address these disclosure issues.

Notable filings include:

- EDGX (order type clarifications / July 25)[2]
- EDGA (order type clarifications / August 11)[3]

---

[2] Notice of Filing of a Proposed Rule Change by EDGX Exchange, Inc. Relating to Include Additional Specificity Within Rule 1.5 and Chapter XI Regarding Current System Functionality Including the Operation of Order Types and Order Instructions, Exchange Act Release No. 72,676, 79 Fed. Reg. 44,520 (July 25, 2014), *available at* http://www.gpo.gov/fdsys/pkg/FR-2014-07-31/pdf/2014-17989.pdf.

[3] Notice of Filing of a Proposed Rule Change by EDGA Exchange, Inc. Relating to Include Additional Specificity Within Rule 1.5 and Chapter XI Regarding Current System Functionality Including the Operation of Order Types and Order

- BATS (data feeds / July 28)[4]
- BATS Y (data feeds / July 28)[5]
- Chicago Stock Exchange (data feeds / July 29)[6]
- EDGA (data feeds / July 28)[7]
- EDGX (data feeds / July 28)[8]
- NASDAQ OMX BX (data feeds / July 29)[9]

Instructions, Exchange Act Release No. 72,812, 79 Fed. Reg. 48,824, 48,824 (Aug. 11, 2014), *available at* http://www.gpo.gov/fdsys/pkg/FR-2014-08-18/pdf/2014-19415.pdf.

[4] Notice of Filing and Immediate Effectiveness of a Proposed Rule Change by BATS Exchange, Inc. to Clarify for Members and Non-Members the Use of Certain Data Feeds for Order Handling and Execution, Order Routing and Regulatory Compliance, Exchange Act Release No. 72,685, 79 Fed. Reg. 44,889 (July 28, 2014), *available at* http://www.gpo.gov/fdsys/pkg/FR-2014-08-01/pdf/2014-18120.pdf.

[5] Notice of Filing and Immediate Effectiveness of a Proposed Rule Change by BATS Y-Exchange, Inc. to Clarify for Members and Non-Members the Use of Certain Data Feeds for Order Handling and Execution, Order Routing and Regulatory Compliance, Exchange Act Release No. 72,687, 79 Fed. Reg. 44,926 (July 28, 2014), *available at* http://www.gpo.gov/fdsys/pkg/FR-2014-08-01/pdf/2014-18122.pdf.

[6] Notice of Filing and Immediate Effectiveness of a Proposed Rule Change by Chicago Stock Exchange, Inc. Concerning the Use of Market Data Feeds by the Exchange, Exchange Act Release No. 72,711, 79 Fed. Reg. 45,570 (July 29, 2014), *available at* http://www.gpo.gov/fdsys/pkg/FR-2014-08-05/pdf/2014-18385.pdf.

[7] Notice of Filing and Immediate Effectiveness of a Proposed Rule Change by EDGA Exchange, Inc. to Clarify for Members and Non-Members the Use of Certain Data Feeds for Order Handling and Execution, Order Routing and Regulatory Compliance, Exchange Act Release No. 72,682, 79 Fed. Reg. 44,938 (July 28, 2014), *available at* http://www.gpo.gov/fdsys/pkg/FR-2014-08-01/pdf/2014-18117.pdf.

[8] Notice of Filing and Immediate Effectiveness of a Proposed Rule Change by EDGX Exchange, Inc. to Clarify for Members and Non-Members the Use of Certain Data Feeds for Order Handling and Execution, Order Routing and Regulatory Compliance, Exchange Act Release No. 72,683, 79 Fed. Reg. 44,950 (July 28, 2014), *available at* http://www.gpo.gov/fdsys/pkg/FR-2014-08-01/pdf/2014-18118.pdf.

[9] Notice of Filing and Immediate Effectiveness of a Proposed Rule Change by NASDAQ OMX BX, Inc. to Disclose Publicly the Sources of Data Used for Exchange Functions, Exchange Act Release No. 72,712, 79 Fed. Reg. 45,521 (July 29, 2014), *available at* http://www.gpo.gov/fdsys/pkg/FR-2014-08-05/pdf/2014-18386.pdf.

- NASDAQ OMX PHLX (data feeds / July 29)[10]
- NASDAQ (data feeds / July 28)[11]
- NYSE (data feeds / July 29)[12]
- NYSE MKT (data feeds / July 29)[13]
- NYSE Arca (data feeds / July 29)[14]

Also consider the order type statistics now made available by exchanges as a direct result of the order type controversy, including NYSE Arca Order Type Usage[15] and BATS Order Type Usage Summary.[16] For an example of an undocumented order type evident in these statistics, I would single out the Post Only ISO order type

---

[10] Notice of Filing and Immediate Effectiveness of a Proposed Rule Change by NASDAQ OMX PHLX LLC to Disclose Publicly the Sources of Data Used for Exchange Functions, Exchange Act Release No. 72,713, 79 Fed. Reg. 45,544 (July 29, 2014), *available at* http://www.gpo.gov/fdsys/pkg/FR-2014-08-05/pdf/2014-18387.pdf.

[11] Notice of Filing and Immediate Effectiveness of Proposed Rule Change by NASDAQ Stock Market LLC to Disclose Publicly the Sources of Data Used for Exchange Functions, Exchange Act Release No. 72,684, 79 Fed. Reg. 44,956 (July 28, 2014), *available at* http://www.gpo.gov/fdsys/pkg/FR-2014-08-01/pdf/2014-18119.pdf.

[12] Notice of Filing and Immediate Effectiveness of a Proposed Rule Change by New York Stock Exchange LLC Clarifying the Exchange's Use of Certain Data Feeds for Order Handling and Execution, Order Routing, and Regulatory Compliance, Exchange Act Release No. 72,710, 79 Fed. Reg. 45,511 (July 29, 2014), *available at* http://www.gpo.gov/fdsys/pkg/FR-2014-08-05/pdf/2014-18384.pdf.

[13] Notice of Filing and Immediate Effectiveness of a Proposed Rule Change by NYSE MKT LLC Clarifying the Exchange's Use of Certain Data Feeds for Order Handling and Execution, Order Routing, and Regulatory Compliance, Exchange Act Release No. 72,709, 79 Fed. Reg. 45,513 (July 29, 2014), *available at* http://www.gpo.gov/fdsys/pkg/FR-2014-08-05/pdf/2014-18383.pdf.

[14] Notice of Filing and Immediate Effectiveness of a Proposed Rule Change by NYSE Arca, Inc. Clarifying the Exchange's Use of Certain Data Feeds for Order Handling and Execution, Order Routing, and Regulatory Compliance, Exchange Act Release No. 72,708, 79 Fed. Reg. 45.572 (July 29, 2014), *available at* http://www.gpo.gov/fdsys/pkg/FR-2014-08-05/pdf/2014-18382.pdf.

[15] *Order Type Usage (Percentage of Matched Volume)*, NYSE ARCA, https://www.nyse.com/publicdocs/nyse/markets/nyse-arca/NYSE_Arca_Order_Type_Usage.pdf (last visited Aug. 20, 2014).

[16] *Order Type Usage Summary*, BATS, http://batstrading.com/market_data/order_types/ (last visited Aug. 20, 2014).

as an advanced order type central to HFT strategies and implemented on the major exchanges. This order type, which typically ranges between 4%-8% of such metrics, is woefully incomplete in meeting disclosure requirements, and the situation requires a meaningful resolution. For certain exchanges, one might not even be able verify that the Post Only ISO order type is supported by the trading venue in question without referring to the odd disclosure made available through these order type statistics.

Another concern evident in the order type statistics is the broad bifurcation between classes of market participants and order types developed for such classes. More strikingly, not only are such percentages on the order type usage consistent with my claim that HFT-oriented order types are central to exchange volume,[17] but the statistics also show that a significant proportion of trading activity continues to use investor-oriented order types that interact in a non-transparent manner with HFT order types. In other words, the buy-side and their sell-side brokers are still behind the curve in leveraging the advanced order types to better serve their clients.

Of course, these statistics are entirely consistent with how exchanges have managed their business development process—we have had a two-tier system for quite a while. In fact, the segmentation of the customer base along the lines of HFT and non-HFT and the general practice of developing features that accommodate the two classes separately goes back to the early years of the HFT industry. This practice was quite accurately described by current BATS CEO Joe Ratterman back in 2005 when the industry was shifting its practices to emphasize high-speed trading:

> *"The markets have evolved and the current playing field doesn't cater as well as it could for today's market players. Our goal is to provide a new set of interfaces and trading paradigms that suits both the short-term liquidity providers*

---

[17] *See* HAIM BODEK, THE PROBLEM OF HFT: COLLECTED WRITINGS ON HIGH FREQUENCY TRADING & STOCK MARKET STRUCTURE REFORM (2013), *available at* http://www.amazon.com/gp/product/B00B1UDSS4.

> *as well as the traditional investing and trading community. Our aim is to focus on the individual needs of each market group, while bringing these players together in a new trading arena.*"[18]

By now, it should be clear to the informed reader that the order type interaction between "short-term liquidity providers" and the "traditional trading and investing community" becomes a central concern when the two broad groups are brought together in "a new trading arena." Are both segments adequately informed when they come into the same venue? Do they truly have access to the same toolset in any practical sense? Whether by design or agreement or understanding, does one set of participants leverage exchange features to the detriment of the other class? If asymmetries exist in the market, are they properly disclosed?

In other words, have exchanges been forthright in providing accurate operating manuals to their customers and to the SEC? (Recent submissions alone lead to the inference that adequate disclosure has been lacking over much of the high-speed trading era.) Do exchanges monitor the impact of order matching practices and order types upon their membership? And if they see members falling victim to the "tricks of the trade," do they intervene to protect investors? Are exchanges acting as unbiased referees and maintaining a level playing field? To what degree are they even obligated to do so, given their for-profit motives? These are the central questions of the order type controversy.

Despite the progress on disclosure evident in the recent rule filings, I remain critical of many of these "clarifications," some of which seem to indicate backpedaling, weak justifications, or further attempts to get away with minimal disclosure of the features I have heavily criticized. Still, these filings represent progress, and I am

---

[18] Press Release, BATS Trading, Inc., BATS Trading, Inc. Is Formed 1 (June 17, 2005), http://www.batstrading.com/resources/press_releases/BATS%20Trading%20is%20Formed.pdf.

happy that these issues are finally being submitted to the regulators with improved transparency. With the October deadline imposed on securities exchanges for internal reviews of order type practices[19] and the Wall Street Journal reporting on negotiations between regulators and a major securities exchange,[20] the progress so far is promising.

In the meantime, I encourage all stakeholders on both sides of the order type debate to review the recent exchange submissions and submit comments to the SEC. Some of these comment letters will have my name on them.

---

[19] *Oversight of the SEC's Division of Trading and Markets: Hearing Before the Subcomm. on Capital Mkts. & Gov't Sponsored Enters. of the H. Comm. on Fin. Servs.*, 113th Cong. 28 (2014), available at http://www.gpo.gov/fdsys/pkg/CHRG-113hhrg91152/pdf/CHRG-113hhrg91152.pdf (remarks of Stephen Luparello, Director, Division of Trading and Markets, U.S. Securities and Exchange Commission).

[20] Bradley Hope et al., *BATS to Settle High-Speed Trading Case*, WALL ST. J. (Aug. 5, 2014), http://www.wsj.com/articles/bats-to-settle-high-speed-trading-case-1407284108.

III. Deconstructing Maker-Taker

Haim Bodek and Stanislav Dolgopolov
Decimus Capital Markets, LLC
June–July 2014
Originally appeared online in *Tabb Forum*

A. A Gordian Knot for Market Structure?

The maker-taker pricing model, a seemingly innocuous financial innovation that draws the line between "makers" and "takers" of liquidity—via a maze of rebates and fees—has become a Gordian knot for the current market structure. Being on the frontline of regulatory debates, this pricing model was the real star of the recent Senate hearing,[1] and this very fact elevates the awareness of the market structure crisis to a whole new level.

Needless to say, this financial innovation got little love from Michael Lewis in his "Flash Boys": "The maker-taker system of fees and kickbacks used by all [sic] of the exchanges was simply a method for paying the big Wall Street banks to screw the investors whose interests they were meant to guard."[2] While we certainly do not subscribe to this generalization, it is hard to disagree that "Flash Boys"—also repeatedly referred to during the Senate hearing—galvanized a truly national debate on controversial payoff structures in securities markets.

The maker-taker pricing model is both a byproduct and a cause of fragmentation, which is a much-feared trend nowadays. This

---

[1] *Conflicts of Interest, Investor Loss of Confidence, and High Speed Trading in U.S. Stock Markets, Hearing Before the Permanent Subcomm. on Investigations of the S. Comm. on Homeland Sec. & Governmental Affairs*, 113th Cong. (2014), available at http://www.gpo.gov/fdsys/pkg/CHRG-113shrg89752/pdf/CHRG-113shrg89752.pdf.

[2] MICHAEL LEWIS, FLASH BOYS: A WALL STREET REVOLT 168–69 (2014).

model's origins can be traced to the late 1990s, with the emergence of new trading venues, such as Island ECN, which resorted to innovation in order to attract order flow. Going forward, trading venues now employ the maker-taker pricing model as a means of a multifaceted segmentation for market participants with specific trading strategies. Beyond the race to the highest liquidity rebate or the lowest access fee, this trend has led to the emergence of new trading venues—sometimes with multiple platforms under the same roof—with different pricing structures, including "inverted" ones. Furthermore, a trading venue may keep a portion of the liquidity rebate or, in some cases, even subsidize volume by providing the liquidity rebate exceeding the access fee.

The maker-taker pricing model is often characterized—quite correctly—as a form of compensation for "adverse selection" offered to traders exposing nonmarketable limit orders. However, in that respect and several others, this pricing model is a creature of the applicable tick-size regime. As the tick size gets smaller, the real impact of given maker-taker arrangements diminishes. This relationship explains why an access fee or a liquidity rebate is typically smaller than one tick, although certain stocks quoted in sub-pennies are a notable exception.

Moreover, maker-taker arrangements often result in a bigger bang for low-priced stocks or when the underlying bid-ask spread is only one tick wide, as fees and rebates are applied on the per-share basis. Yes, the existence of a wide range of "regular" and "inverted" fee-rebate structures undoes—to some extent—the minimum pricing variation rule and raises concerns related to the order protection rule, with both of these rules set by Regulation NMS. Furthermore, it would not be easy to incorporate such adjustments into public quotes directly, given the sheer complexity of such fee-rebate structures.

Generally, the maker-taker pricing model does provide an incentive to post orders in addition to incentives feasible under the price grid in question. On the other hand, practices coming under the umbrella of "rebate arbitrage," which generate profits primarily from collecting liquidity rebates, are frequently criticized as "ephemeral liquidity." To add to the mix, this pricing model is compatible with the existence of designated market makers, which may receive greater liquidity rebates compared to everyone else in exchange for trading obligations. In other words, maker-taker arrangements and mechanisms of liquidity provision are closely related, but trading venues' business models, market maker programs, and order flow characteristics are of great importance.

The maker-taker pricing model is often favorably contrasted to an alternative allocation mechanism, payment for order flow. Yet, while market-taker arrangements are frequently praised as "democratic," "nondiscriminatory," and "transparent," some of them are not unlike their much-criticized cousin. As an example, tiered fees and rebates employed by many trading venues are not egalitarian even on the surface.

While volume discounts as such are in no way problematic, there are concerns that at least some of these "mega tiers" (an official term in some instances) are structured in an anticompetitive way. More specifically, one scenario to consider is whether HFT profit margins converge to the differential between regular and mega tiers. To rephrase the question: Are otherwise efficient liquidity providers driven out by the underlying pricing structure?

As another similarity with payment for order flow practices, certain fee-rebate structures are hard to describe as transparent, given their indecipherable and poorly documented mechanics. Sometimes, even the very process of determination of who would be a "maker" and who would be a "taker" lacks transparency, especially in cases where price-sliding practices have significant impact on order handling. Furthermore, such fee-rebate structures are typically used in conjunction with certain order types (and this topic has been extensively discussed by Mr. Bodek[3]).

The securities industry has admitted the existence of the link between the maker-taker pricing model and the expanding universe

---

[3] *See* HAIM BODEK, THE PROBLEM OF HFT: COLLECTED WRITINGS ON HIGH FREQUENCY TRADING & STOCK MARKET STRUCTURE REFORM (2013), *available at* http://www.amazon.com/gp/product/B00B1UDSS4.

of order types, although this link is often framed in terms of its contribution to the growing level of complexity of securities markets. As articulated in the Senate testimony by Thomas W. Farley, who represents the next generation of the New York Stock Exchange's leadership, eliminating the maker-taker pricing model "would reduce the conflicts inherent in such pricing schema and further reduce complexity through fewer order types and fewer venues."[4] In her recent speech, Mary Jo White, the SEC's Chairman, also pointed to the fact that many order types "are designed to deal with the maker-taker fee model and the SEC's rule against locking quotations" and requested trading venues "to conduct a comprehensive review of their order types and how they operate in practice."[5]

Clearly, the implications of the maker-taker pricing model for the current market structure must be unraveled in order to achieve a comprehensive reform of securities markets. It is increasingly hard to dismiss the proposition that the overall burden this pricing model has placed upon the regulatory, technological, and trading functions of the marketplace as a whole might in fact outweigh its benefits. While the authors are not ready to cut this Gordian knot in half by doing away with the maker-taker pricing model altogether, we certainly sympathize with the viewpoint that the utility of this model must be challenged, lest it continue to play an incumbent role in the post-crisis market structure.

B. Time to Cut the Knot?

One major problem embedded in the maker-taker pricing model reveals itself in the context of agency transactions. The generally valid claim asserts that the pricing model distorts brokers'

---

[4] *Hearing on Conflicts of Interest, Investor Loss of Confidence, and High Speed Trading in U.S. Stock Markets*, *supra* note, at 32 (prepared statement of Thomas W. Farley, President, New York Stock Exchange).

[5] Mary Jo White, Chairman, U.S. Sec. & Exch. Comm'n, Enhancing Our Equity Market Structure: Remarks at Sandler O'Neill & Partners, L.P. Global Exchange and Brokerage Conference (June 5, 2014), http://www.sec.gov/News/Speech/Detail/Speech/1370542004312#.U99FBGN5WEc.

incentives. The nature of this distortion is traced to brokers' business practices—they often charge their customers an all-inclusive brokerage commission and get to keep liquidity rebates, while also bearing the penalty of access fees.

To generate higher margins on the spread between their fixed brokerage commissions and variable execution costs, brokers may be tempted to balance fees and rebates at the expense of their customers. This harm—accompanied by violations of the duty of best execution owed by brokers to their customers—may manifest itself under a number of scenarios, which have been extensively discussed by other commentators and analyzed in a high-profile empirical study.[6] There are strong arguments that brokers' practices to optimize fees and rebates run directly opposed to maximizing price-improvement opportunities and fill rates.

Another consideration is that brokers can bifurcate their order flow by separately optimizing the economics of marketable and nonmarketable orders in order to "double-dip." For example, a broker can sell marketable orders to wholesalers (instead of paying access fees) and route nonmarketable orders to trading venues (and collect liquidity rebates). As an illustration, during a recent Senate hearing, an executive of a leading brokerage firm admitted that his firm gets paid for agency orders in one of these two ways on "nearly every trade."[7]

The real problem isn't even that brokers get paid either way—unless these arrangements are not adequately disclosed to customers—but whether either category of orders could have been executed more effectively. In any instance, this scrutiny of order routing nuances on the level of the U.S. Senate puts the securities industry on notice that the optimization of brokers' profit margins will be assessed with regard to adverse impact on execution quality. Could this discussion

---

[6] Robert Battalio et al., Can Brokers Have It All? On the Relation between Make-Take Fees and Limit Order Execution Quality (Mar. 5, 2014) (unpublished manuscript), *available at* http://ssrn.com/abstract=2367462.
[7] *Hearing on Conflicts of Interest, Investor Loss of Confidence, and High Speed Trading in U.S. Stock Markets*, *supra* note, at 45 (answer of Steven Quick, Senior Vice President, Trader Group, TD Ameritrade).

mark the end of the common misperception—already refuted by the courts and regulators—that the duty of best execution is achieved simply by executing at or within the National Best Bid and Offer?

In any instance, is there a regulatory remedy to preempt order routing practices that tempt brokers to violate the duty of best execution out of self-interest? A seemingly simple solution of a mandatory pass-through of fees and rebates to customers has many complications, such as the existence of tiered pricing and difficulties with ex post allocation. Furthermore, such pass-through arrangements have not become dominant as a contractual feature in brokerage agreements for a reason. After all, retail investors tend to be "takers" of liquidity, and an all-inclusive brokerage commission has a lot of appeal to this group for the sake of simplicity.

Likewise, implementing a pass-through mechanism presents a great operational challenge for—and hence is eschewed by—many traditional institutional investors, as they would have to allocate net amounts among different funds/subaccounts. On the other hand, pass-through arrangements are offered by brokers to hedge funds, which often have a simple investment structure, and non-broker-dealer HFTs, which may engage in maker-taker-based trading strategies and frequently rely on sponsored access. Notably, one could run a top-notch HFT strategy with a wrong broker-dealer, which fails to make it to the mega tier, and end up with zero margin. A more pressing concern—and a more difficult one to detect—is whether a pass-through mechanism itself could be abused by an unfaithful broker.

One thing worth mentioning about distortions introduced by the maker-taker pricing model is that resulting violations of the duty of best execution are a species of securities fraud. As analyzed in a forthcoming article by one of the authors, the link between certain maker-taker-related practices and securities fraud is even wider, extending to both agency and principal trading.[8] For instance, given

---

[8] Stanislav Dolgopolov, *The Maker-Taker Pricing Model and Its Impact on the Securities Market Structure: A Can of Worms for Securities Fraud?*, 8 VA. L. & BUS. REV. 231 (2014), *available at* http://ssrn.com/abstract=2399821.

the criticism that rebate arbitrage is "distortionary" and "artificial," do any trading strategies in this category fit the legal definition of market manipulation or any other type of securities fraud? What is the extent of liability of trading venues and certain market participants in connection with nontransparent fee-rebate structures, including complex order types? What legal hook could catch a designated market maker benefiting from a preferential fee-rebate structure if that market participant deliberately fails to meet its trading obligations?

Questions like this are no longer a theoretical exercise. A far-reaching class action is now targeting a broad gamut of defendants, with securities fraud as the lynchpin.[9] In addition to the best execution perspective, the complaint essentially characterizes rebate arbitrage as fraudulent, alleges that certain maker-taker-based trading strategies cause price movements unfavorable to other market participants, and attacks complex order types.

Looking forward, what course of action should be taken? It appears that not all proposed regulatory fixes appreciate numerous nuances of the maker-taker pricing model and its interlacement with other market structure pillars—be it fragmentation, payment for order flow, or the tick size regime, including price grids used by dark pools and wholesalers. Abolishing this pricing model through government intervention might be a brave move, but doing a pilot study first, an option seriously considered by the regulators in United States and Canada, is a better move. A related question to ponder is whether a complete ban will lead to the emergence of similar, if not shadier, payoff structures.

One reform proposal to consider is lowering the cap on access fees and hence scaling down liquidity rebates, with the caveat that some trading venues fund liquidity rebates from a variety of sources. Individual trading venues may be reluctant to lower their access fees unilaterally, as the current situation could be described—with a fair degree of accuracy—as a "race to the cap."

---

[9] Complaint for Violation of the Federal Securities Laws, City of Providence, R.I. v. BATS Global Mkts., Inc., No. 1:14-cv-2811 (S.D.N.Y. Apr. 18, 2014).

In any instance, the current fee cap of 0.3 cents per share was set as a de facto standard in the securities industry back in 2005—during a very different era. In fact, Douglas Cifu, the CEO of Virtu Financial, a leading HFT firm that focuses on market making, recently suggested that even 0.05 cents per share would work without interfering with the function of providing liquidity.[10] Moreover, this fee cap applies only to equity securities, and one of the authors had expressed his support for the SEC's proposed—and ultimately abandoned—measure to impose a similar cap in options markets.[11]

At the end, macro solutions should not distract from scrutinizing and shedding more light on specific fee-rebate mechanisms—a path that is getting more and more traffic. If we are to call the maker-taker pricing model "democratic," "transparent," and "nondiscriminatory," let us walk the walk. Anticompetitive effects of tiered pricing need to be examined—with the realization that more complicated pricing structures may be useful in certain circumstances, for instance, in order to promote meaningful market making obligations.

Nontransparent maker-taker arrangements and related order types practices also need more scrutiny. The securities industry is already cleaning up this corner, and the regulators are on the trail. As an illustration, during yet another congressional hearing touching on the market structure crisis, Stephen Luparello, the Director of the SEC's Division of Trading and Markets, articulated that "[m]aker-taker in certain areas of the market is definitely tied inextricably to the growth of complex order types" and described the regulatory agency's focus on "whether or not those order types are consistent

---

[10] Panel: Market Structure I, Sandler O'Neill Global Exchange and Brokerage (June 4, 2014) (remarks of Douglas Cifu, Chief Executive Officer, Virtu Financial LLC).

[11] Letter from Haim Bodek, Chief Exec. Officer, Trading Machines LLC, to Mary Shapiro, Chairman, U.S. Sec. & Exch. Comm'n (June 21, 2010), *available at* http://www.sec.gov/comments/s7-09-10/s70910-22.pdf.

with how they were described to us in the first instance."[12] Finally, as mentioned by Mary Jo White, the SEC's Chairman, in connection with maker-taker and payment for order flow arrangements, the regulatory agency is considering "a rule that would enhance order routing disclosures" made by brokers,[13] and this measure might prove to be another step in the direction of transparency.

While the authors believe it is time to cut the Gordian knot of the maker-taker pricing model, we do not propose to do so by eliminating maker-taker altogether. While the hard problems described above will undoubtedly burden the securities industry, regulators, and courts for some time to come, it is possible to lessen the degree of damage. To that end, we think that slashing the current fee cap by two-thirds to 0.1 cents per share is a compelling and reasonable solution for reigning in maker-taker distortions and limiting the adverse impact of conflicts of interest created by order routing practices.

---

[12] *Oversight of the SEC's Division of Trading and Markets: Hearing Before the Subcomm. on Capital Mkts. & Gov't Sponsored Enters. of the H. Comm. on Fin. Servs.*, 113th Cong. 28 (2014), *available at* http://www.gpo.gov/fdsys/pkg/CHRG-113hhrg91152/pdf/CHRG-113hhrg91152.pdf (remarks of Stephen Luparello, Director, Division of Trading and Markets, U.S. Securities and Exchange Commission).

[13] White, Enhancing Our Equity Market Structure, *supra* note.

IV. The Problem of Fragmentation and Potential Solutions

Haim Bodek and Stanislav Dolgopolov
Decimus Capital Markets, LLC
October 2015
Adopted from *The Market Structure Crisis in the U.S. Securities Industry in 2015 and Beyond* **(a proprietary research report available from Decimus Capital Markets, LLC)**

One of the pivotal concepts in market structure is the one of "fragmentation," which is generally associated with complexities and uncertainties in executing across the multitude of trading venues that comprise the modern electronic marketplace. The term "fragmentation" often has a negative connotation, or, on the other end of the spectrum, it is equated with competition and the elimination of single points of failure. More generally, fragmentation simply indicates the existence or the degree of dispersion of trading in the same security across different trading venues. Regulation NMS with its Rule 611, known as the "order-protection rule" or the "trade-through rule," spurred the process of fragmentation, as it allowing new trading venues to jump in and capture a portion of order flow by displaying a better price, but the very existence of competing trading venues certainly predates this regulatory measure. In the equities space, which may be seen as the most fragmented one, there are eleven securities exchanges, dozens of dark pools and other ATSs, and hundreds of off-exchange market makers.

A. Fragmentation as a Debated Issue and a Key Driver of HFT

The very existence of fragmentation presents a number of problems, such an imperfect aggregation of trading interests, a distorted price discovery process, and more opportunities for gaming the system, including inter-venue arbitrage strategies, the problem of fleeting liquidity, and the conflicts of interest that may impact routing broker-dealers, with these scenarios sensationalized in *Flash Boys*. Indeed, in the current market structure crisis, fragmentation is often seen as one of the chief evils by a range of critics from both pro-HFT and anti-HFT camps, although competition in general is ironically heralded as a success by many industry insiders, regulators, and academics. Moreover, many commentators question the social utility of *additional* trading venues regardless of their business models and blame fragmentation for the increasing complexity of the current market structure.[1] In other words, there is a provocative argument that there could be *excessive* competition. In any instance, fragmentation is one of the key drivers of HFT, as players in this space often engage in arbitrage strategies that exploit inter-venue low-latency differentials. Such practices are frequently criticized as unnecessary intermediation, and there are legitimate concerns over ephemeral liquidity and flickering quotes, which may lead to misguided order routing and inferior executions for many investors.

The bottom line is that it is impossible to synchronize the overall architecture of securities markets in continuous time, given the geographic dispersion of trading venues (that is, their matching engines) and market participants themselves. Furthermore, fragmentation cannot be simply regulated out of existence by abolishing competition or *closely* binding different trading venues via a mandatory matching-engine-like protocol. There have been many concerns about the rigidity of a "CLOB" (i.e., a "central limit order book") and its resistance to innovation, with the original

---

[1] *See, e.g.*, FIA PRINCIPAL TRADERS GRP. (FIA PTG), EQUITY MARKET STRUCTURE POSITION PAPER 4 (Sept. 30, 2014), *available at* http://www.futuresindustry.org/ptg/downloads/FIA%20PTG%20Equity%20Market%20Structure%20Postion%20Paper.pdf ("Although venue competition has brought unquestionable benefits in terms of transaction costs and innovation, fragmentation has become excessive and introduced undue complexity to the marketplace. Regulatory policy, including Reg NMS, has facilitated the creation and sustainability of exchanges and other trading venues that could not have survived under normal competitive dynamics. Additional exchanges impose a cost on all market participants.").

proposal dating back to the 1970s, and some of these concerns definitely merit attention. The very process of administering and controlling such a centralized architecture, whether entrusted to the regulators or the securities industry itself, might as well be a cure worse than the disease itself. In other words, fragmentation is here to stay, but it is likely to be tinkered with by the regulators in order to strengthen the notion of a binding National Best Bid and Offer honored by all trading venues and available to all investors. Needless to say, different scenarios of this regulatory intervention will have a real impact on certain industry players and their business models, particularly those dependent on HFT volume.

B. *The Phenomenon of Latency Arbitrage*

One area that has received a lot of attention is the potential adverse impact of latency on investors as a result of market data "race conditions" among trading venues. This phenomenon can be reduced to three basic scenarios: (1) HFTs pulling quotes on trading venues when a single venue is hit in a "sweep" event; (2) an inferior trade when a midpoint / pegging order is priced off the consolidated data feed; and (3) an inferior trade when trading venues are "traded-through" in less than one second, which is permitted by the "one second" exception of Rule 611 of Regulation NMS, i.e., the trade-through rule.[2] These issues have been highlighted in *Flash Boys* and

---

[2] The specific language of this exception is as follows: "The trading center displaying the protected quotation that was traded through had displayed, within one second prior to execution of the transaction that constituted the trade-through, a best bid or best offer, as applicable, for the NMS stock with a price that was equal or inferior to the price of the trade-through transaction." Regulation NMS, Exchange Act Release No. 51,808, 70 Fed. Reg. 37,496, 37,631 (June 9, 2005) (to be codified at Order Protection Rule, 17 C.F.R. § 240.611(b)(8)), *available at* http://www.gpo.gov/fdsys/pkg/FR-2005-06-29/pdf/05-11802.pdf. More generally, Rule 611 was adopted in 2005, a time period with very different securities markets and technology constraints. *See* Letter from Haim Bodek, Managing Principal, Decimus Capital Mkts., LLC & Peter Kovac, Managing Member, Ozone Park Partners, to Brent J. Fields, Sec'y, U.S. Sec. & Exch. Comm'n 2–4 (May 11, 2015), *available at* https://www.sec.gov/comments/265-29/26529-8.pdf. On the other hand, the SEC observed that "[n]o *exchange* has adopted a rule that would allow it to utilize this exception." Memorandum from

are frequently profiled in connection with upstart IEX, a rising trading venue that seeks to mitigate the impact of some low-latency strategies.

The first scenario may be addressed by special routing techniques (e.g., RBC's Thor) and / or through trading venue-specific cancellation restrictions, such as cancellation fees or, to a lesser extent, minimum order resting times. The second scenario may be addressed by adopting speed bumps that limit predatory trading or, at a minimum, requiring trading venues to price off private data feeds. The third scenario may be controlled through enforcement actions and a modification of the one-second exception in the trade-through rule.

The degree of fragmentation exacerbates the phenomenon of latency arbitrage, creating more opportunities for dislocation with additional trading venues. Quite often, the lowest common denominator (i.e., the slowest trading venue) creates an environment in which typical investors and their brokers are at a disadvantage relative to HFTs that use superior data feeds, co-location, special order types, and regulatory exceptions to avoid the pitfalls described above and in fact benefit from them.

Although all three scenarios have been referred to as "latency arbitrage," perhaps only the third one is worthy of that term. Regardless, there is a lot of regulatory attention on all of these scenarios. It is no surprise that Rule 611 was the subject of the first meeting of the SEC's Equity Market Structure Advisory Committee,[3] which touched on various microstructural issues impacting order handling.

C. The Existence of a Wide Range of Trading Venues

---

the SEC Div. of Trading & Mkts. to the SEC Mkt. Structure Advisory Comm. 18 (April 30, 2015), https://www.sec.gov/spotlight/emsac/memo-rule-611-regulation-nms.pdf (emphasis added).

[3] *See* Press Release No. 2015-70, U.S. Sec. & Exch. Comm'n, SEC Announces Agenda for May 13 Meeting of the Equity Market Structure Advisory Committee (Apr. 17, 2015), http://www.sec.gov/news/pressrelease/2015-70.html.

Today's fragmented architecture of securities markets consists of securities exchanges, ATSs, such as electronic communication networks with displayed orders (a less common phenomenon nowadays) and dark pools with undisplayed quotes and special matching mechanisms, and stand-alone broker-dealers as de facto trading venues. One important clarification is that this description primarily applies to the equities space, with its wide spectrum of trading venues. However, markets in other asset classes, such as futures and options, have regulatory restrictions on off-exchange trading. In other words, the problem of fragmentation is critical in equities markets, but not necessarily in other markets.

Within the equities space, alternative execution channels display a great variation in terms of traded volume, regulatory burdens, transparency, and many other factors. For instance, securities exchanges, which are registered as SROs, have a number of regulatory obligations and privileges, such as guidelines for their private regulatory regimes and limitations of liability.[4] By contrast, ATSs, which belong to a separate regulatory category established by the SEC with the passage of Regulation ATS, have a lighter regulatory burden, including fewer restrictions on order flow discrimination, and essentially are subject to a notice-based regime vis-à-vis the regulators. As another illustration, dark pools have no pre-trade transparency, which distinguishes them from "lit" trading venues with displayed orders, although even players in the latter category may have "hidden liquidity" on the books. Stand-alone broker-dealers, which, however, may simultaneously play the role of registered market makers on securities exchanges, execute transactions off-exchange or sometimes reroute them to other

---

[4] Many securities exchanges delegate certain self-regulatory functions to FINRA, and this process is ongoing. *See, e.g.*, Press Release, CBOE Holdings, Inc., CBOE and C2 Enter into Agreements with FINRA Involving Regulatory Services (Dec. 22, 2014), http://ir.cboe.com/press-releases/2014/dec-22-2014.aspx. At the same time, this arrangement is not necessarily stable. *See, e.g.*, Press Release, NYSE Grp., NYSE Regulation to Perform Market Surveillance, Investigation and Enforcement Program for NYSE Group Exchanges (Oct. 6, 2014), http://ir.theice.com/investors-and-media/press/press-releases/press-release-details/2014/NYSE-Regulation-to-Perform-Market-Surveillance-Investigation-and-Enforcement-Program-for-NYSE-Group-Exchanges/default.aspx.

trading venues. These off-exchange market makers, which are often known as wholesalers / internalizers, typically base their respective business models on trading against their customers' orders or pre-existing arrangements with agency brokerages, as the latter often route their own customers' orders based on contractual arrangements in return for monetary payments. Such practices, often referred to as "payment for order flow," were given a critical look in *Flash Boys*, which was not the first source to do so, given the much older criticisms and private lawsuits. Another important dimension of the problem of fragmentation is that trading venues, including leading exchanges, are competing with individual broker-dealers in some ways by providing ancillary services (e.g., algorithmic solutions), and broker-dealers are naturally wary of such encroachments, which may create additional conflicts of interest.[5]

The very existence of this wide range of execution channels leads to the inevitable problem of an imperfect aggregation and competition among individual orders. More competition among trading venues does not necessarily lead to more competition among individual orders. For instance, dark orders by definition have limited interaction with other orders or indications of interest originating on other trading venues, and payment for order flow arrangements often bypass other execution channels. This problem is also compounded by the fact that certain execution options, such as dark pools and off-exchange market makers, may creatively avoid the price grid (i.e., "tick size") policy established by Regulation NMS, while the burden is higher for securities exchanges. As an illustration, an off-exchange market maker is able to "undercut" a securities exchange by offering a de minimis price improvement

---

[5] *See, e.g., Market Structure: Ensuring Orderly, Efficient, Innovative and Competitive Markets for Issuers and Investors: Hearing Before the Subcomm. on Capital Mkts. & Gov't Sponsored Enters. of the H. Comm. on Fin. Servs.*, 112th Cong. 117 (2013), *available at* http://www.gpo.gov/fdsys/pkg/CHRG-112hhrg76108/pdf/CHRG-112hhrg76108.pdf (prepared testimony of Daniel Mathisson, Head of U.S. Equity Trading, Credit Suisse) ("Exchanges now function as broker-dealers in many ways. For example, Nasdaq recently announced they would compete with broker-dealers by selling execution algorithms, which involve significantly more complex technology than simply crossing stock like the Facebook IPO.").

amounting to subpenny pricing, while this option is only rarely available to an exchange.

D. Different Allocation Mechanisms

The very existence of alternative execution channels for same securities raises the issue of allocation mechanisms, which function in the shadow of Regulation NMS. Two mechanisms that should be singled out are the payment for order flow model and the maker-taker pricing model. Payment for order flow practices amount to monetary inducements paid to brokers for routing their customers' orders to a particular trading venue or market maker. This approach is typically used by off-exchange market makers, constituting the backbone of their respective business models, and it is less common but still found among securities exchanges, notably in the options space. The maker-taker pricing model, a more modern invention dating back to the late 1990s, makes a distinction between "makers" and "takers" of liquidity. In its standard form, this model is a matching mechanism that imposes a fee on "aggressive" orders that "take" liquidity, i.e., market orders and marketable limit orders, and provides a rebate to "passive" orders that "make" liquidity, i.e., non-marketable limit orders, while the trading venue in question, which could even be a dark pool, retains a portion of this fee. Maker-taker variations, which include "inverted" structures that pay "takers" and charge "makers," have in fact been adopted by almost every major exchange in the equities and options segments. Furthermore, the traditional rather than inverted model attracts the bulk of the volume, and one may observe the race to the top among different securities exchanges in order to reach the maximum level of access fees permitted by Regulation NMS, with such fees also serving as the funding base (or at least its major source) for liquidity rebates. This factor also explains why lit markets tend to be costlier to access compared to dark markets.

While payment for order flow and maker-taker practices are often contrasted to each other, they share certain similarities under a range of scenarios. While the maker-taker pricing model has often been praised as "democratic," "transparent," and "nondiscriminatory," some of its variations are not unlike payment for order flow arrangements. As an example, tiered fees and rebates are not egalitarian even on the surface, and there are concerns that *some* of these "mega tiers" (an official term in some instances) are structured in an anticompetitive way. Additionally, certain fee-rebate structures have not been transparent, especially while being used in conjunction with complex order types. Notably, institutional investors as a group that tends to take liquidity seem to remain uneasy about the extent and cost of liquidity provided by the maker-taker pricing model.[6]

E. Segmentation

Another key issue is segmentation, which is closely linked to off-exchange trading. In the context of the raging debates about the current market structure, segmentation refers to the feature of separation of orders submitted by different types of market participants and their execution on different trading venues. The chief manifestation of segmentation is the distinction between professional and retail orders. While orders in the latter category are often considered to be "dumb," "neutral," and, ideally, self-offsetting, orders in the former category are considered to be "smart" / "directional" (although not necessarily based on any true inside information), "opportunistic," and one-sided. Terms used to describe professional order flow, which is typically eschewed off-exchange and consequently routed to securities exchanges, include "toxic" and "exhaust," and, conversely, retail orders are coveted by off-exchange market makers and certain dark pools.

Numerous commentators have expressed the concern that lit markets, i.e., securities exchanges, are becoming dominated by toxic order flow, as retail orders are often executed by off-exchange market makers or inside dark pools. Another concern addresses the

---

[6] *See, e.g.*, Letter from Ari Burstein, Assoc. Gen. Counsel, Inv. Co. Inst., to Brent Fields, Sec'y, U.S. Sec. & Exch. Comm'n 4 (May 11, 2015), *available at* http://www.sec.gov/comments/265-29/26529-10.pdf ("If the current incentives for making routing decisions based on the availability and amount of liquidity rebates offered, and access fees charged, by trading venues are reduced or eliminated, we believe a number of benefits to the markets would be brought to bear.").

perceived lack of interaction between marketable orders submitted by retail customers and non-marketable orders submitted by the same group, as orders in the first category are typically sold to off-exchange market makers that have the option of trading against such orders without competition, while orders in the second category are often routed to securities exchanges to obtain a liquidity rebate that is often retained by a broker rather than remitted to a customer. To paraphrase, there is an additional layer of segmentation with respect to different order types of retail investors. A common suggestion is to reverse this segmentation-related trend and bring retail orders back to securities exchanges by placing substantial constraints on off-exchange trading via government regulation and thus effectively disrupting order flow relationships.[7] Some commentators doubt that reversing segmentation would benefit markets overall, and the perceived danger lies in a transfer of wealth from retail to professional traders.[8] In any instance, securities exchanges themselves are attempting to court and retain retail order flow through market-based means, including self-identification, and one illustration is the recently introduced retail price improvement feature.[9]

---

[7] *See, e.g.*, ROUNDTABLE ON EQUITY MARKET STRUCTURE, PANEL II: CREATING A LEVEL PLAYING FIELD FOR EQUITY MARKET PARTICIPANTS (May 13, 2013), *available at* http://www.youtube.com/watch?v=BBm7YZ73lqk (remarks of Gary Katz, President and Chief Executive Officer of International Securities Exchange, LLC) (arguing that the consolidation of order flow on lit exchanges would dilute "exhaust" order flow and "take us further away from a fragile lit market to a more robust market") (34:33–35:09).

[8] *See, e.g.*, BROOKINGS INST., TRADING STOCKS IN AMERICA: KEY POLICY ISSUES 65 (Jan. 30, 2014), http://www.brookings.edu/~/media/events/2014/1/30%20trading%20stocks/201 40130_trading_stocks_transcript.pdf (remarks of Jamil Nazarali, Head of Citadel Execution Services, Citadel Securities) ("If you forced everything on a lit venue where everyone would get the same price you would have a huge transfer of wealth from retail investors to institutional investors because [your] average spread would be the weighted average of both the retail and institutional which would mean institutional clients would get slightly better prices and retail clients would get worse prices.").

[9] *See, e.g.*, Order Approving a Proposed Rule Change by NASDAQ Stock Market LLC to Establish the Retail Price Improvement Program on a Pilot Basis, Exchange Act Release No. 68,937, 78 Fed. Reg. 12,397 (Feb. 15, 2013), *available at* http://www.gpo.gov/fdsys/pkg/FR-2013-02-22/pdf/2013-04096.pdf.

F. Regulatory Controls on Fragmentation

Given the pivotal importance of fragmentation in the equities space, it is important to address different regulatory channels for controlling this factor, as well as their consequences and chances for adoption. Technically, the SEC exercises control over registration of securities exchanges, and, by contrast, the process for ATSs is essentially notice-based. In other words, while some aspects of fragmentation could be regulated *directly* (e.g., by capping the number of exchange "medallions"), it is unlikely to be an effective (or politically feasible) tool. The regulators are much more likely to address concerns over fragmentation indirectly. One such approach is to revisit Rule 611 of Regulation NMS, i.e., the trade-through rule protecting *displayed* top-of-the-book quotations. This rule had encouraged the emergence of high-speed competition, although it might be difficult to reverse the emphasis on low-latency trading strategies and connectivity in the marketplace. For instance, some commentators suggest that minor trading venues might be permitted to be ignored (e.g., in terms of maintaining connectivity) for the purposes of compliance with the trade-through rule.[10]

A different proposal to control fragmentation would grant individual issuers the right to decide on specific trading venues for transactions in their securities or otherwise limit trading of a given security to one location. For instance, there have been calls to confine the process of trading shares of emerging / smaller-cap companies to a single trading venue, presumably picked by issuers themselves, in order to concentrate liquidity and provide incentives for market makers. This proposal has some support among the ranks of the

---

[10] *See, e.g.*, Letter from Theodore R. Lazo, Managing Dir. & Assoc. Gen. Counsel, Sec. Indus. & Fin. Mkts. Ass'n, to Mary Jo White, Chairman, U.S. Sec. & Exch. Comm'n 2 (Oct. 24, 2014), *available at* http://www.sec.gov/comments/s7-02-10/s70210-422.pdf ("SIFMA recommends that the displayed quotations of a market center should not be protected under Regulation NMS unless the market center provides substantial liquidity to the market over a sustained period of time.").

SEC's leadership[11] and some key exchanges.[12] Finally, as a unilateral concentration-related initiative in the less liquid segment, the BATS–Direct Edge group of securities exchanges adopted a softer policy that these exchanges "may determine not to designate for trading any security admitted to unlisted trading privileges that does not meet certain consolidated average daily trading volume thresholds."[13] The articulated rationales included the assertions that "liquidity providers will have an incentive to quote more competitively because concentrating the quoted liquidity on the listing exchange would: (i) reduce liquidity providers' risk of adverse selection when quoting in a fragmented market; (ii) provide greater certainty of execution on the one exchange at which liquidity providers are quoting; and (iii) enhance competition for order book priority at the national best bid or offer and throughout the depth of book."[14]

---

[11] *See, e.g.*, Daniel M. Gallagher, Comm'r, U.S. Sec. & Exch. Comm'n, Whatever Happened to Promoting Small Business Capital Formation? Remarks at the Institute for Economic Freedom and Opportunity, The Heritage Foundation (Sept. 17, 2014), http://www.sec.gov/News/Speech/Detail/Speech/1370542976550#.VCFCoBb4XQh ("I've called for the creation of 'Venture Exchanges': national exchanges, with trading and listing rules tailored for smaller companies, including those engaging in issuances under Regulation A. . . . The exchanges themselves would be exempted from the Commission's national market structure and unlisted trading privileges rules, so as to concentrate liquidity in these venues.").

[12] *See, e.g.*, Statement of Thomas Wittman, Executive Vice President, NASDAQ OMX Group, Inc., Equity Market Structure Advisory Committee Meeting 5 (May 13, 2015), https://www.sec.gov/comments/265-29/26529-14.pdf ("Affording . . . small companies the option to suspend unlisted trading privileges in their securities would deepen liquidity and re-ignite competition among orders by focusing all trading onto a single platform. To the extent that this competition results in improved spreads and deeper liquidity, smaller companies electing this option could enjoy many benefits, including reduced capital costs.").

[13] Order Approving Proposed Rule Changes by BATS Exchange, Inc., BATS Y-Exchange, Inc., EDGA Exchange, Inc., and EDGX Exchange, Inc. Relating to Liquidity Requirements for Securities Admitted to Unlisted Trading Privileges, Exchange Act Release No. 75,354, 80 Fed. Reg. 39,462, 39,462 (July 2, 2015), *available at* http://www.gpo.gov/fdsys/pkg/FR-2015-07-09/pdf/2015-16727.pdf.

[14] *Id.*

Another indirect approach to fragmentation lays in tweaking the maker-taker pricing model, perhaps as a means for the regulators to put an end to the collective action problem of the race to the maximum access fee. Going beyond the process of providing the highest liquidity rebate or the lowest access fee, trading venues employ this model, which is often fused with complex order types, as a means of a multifaceted segmentation for market participants with specific trading strategies. This segmentation includes radically different order handling procedures and economics if rebate-sensitive traders who post liquidity are to be compared with fee-incurring removers of liquidity. Accordingly, this trend has led to the emergence of new trading venues with different pricing structures, including inverted ones, and, quite often, multiple platforms are under the same roof of a major exchange group, such as BATS–Direct Edge. Possible efforts to ban maker-taker arrangements entirely, an unlikely option, or to impose price controls for access fees or liquidity rebates, a more likely scenario, could put some trading venues out of business or at least decrease their value proposition. For instance, in the current environment, many dark pools have lower access fees compared to securities exchanges, and a decreased access fee cap, potentially effected via a modification to Regulation NMS, would threaten these dark pools' ability to compete.[15] This scenario also illustrates the existing disparity among trading venues in connection with pricing models and the impact of regulation, inviting a holistic approach.

G. Attacks on Dark Liquidity and the Trade-At Rule

Vocal demands to curtail, if not abolish, dark liquidity / off-exchange trading are often heard from securities exchanges, dark pools' natural competitors. This criticism often cites regulatory advantages enjoyed by dark pools and alleges detrimental market-

---

[15] For instance, an executive of a leading market making firm suggested that the existing access fee cap is "a huge incentive to build dark pools" and its reduction would "dramatically diminish[] the incentive" to create and trade in dark pools. Sam Mamudi, *Flawed Fee Model Distorts U.S. Trading, Virtu Says*, BLOOMBERG (Jan. 2, 2014), http://www.bloomberg.com/news/2014-01-02/flawed-fee-model-distorts-u-s-tradingvirtu-s-concannon-says.html (quoting Chris Concannon, executive vice president, Virtu Financial LLC).

wide effects of dark liquidity, such as piggybacking on the price discovery process implicit in visible quotes. Any restrictions imposed on dark pools would of course draw order flow back to securities exchanges, although trading venues in the latter category often have their own "hidden" order types or subpenny pricing (e.g., as a component of the applicable retail liquidity program). Similarly, market makers functioning primarily on lit exchanges would be able to profit at the expense of their counterparts providing liquidity off-exchange. On the other hand, market players operating on exchanges may use dark pools to offload some of their risks, but the overall decline in the usage of dark pools may compensate for this risk-management device. Similarly, securities exchanges often criticize the model employed by off-exchange market makers, given the frequent usage of subpenny pricing and the exclusivity of order flow arrangements, which is often equated—for good reasons—to insulation from competitive pressures.

Adopting a version of the much talked-about "trade-at" rule is certainly one way to tilt the competitive landscape in favor of securities exchanges. In any instance, the broad concept of trade-at is that orders should be executed against displayed quotations instead of being diverted to / passively matched by other trading venues / off-exchange unless there is an economically meaningful price improvement. In fact, this controversial measure was suggested by the NYSE, NASDAQ, and BATS to solve the problem of dark liquidity.[16] The trade-at rule is a significant threat to dark

---

[16] NASDAQ OMX GRP., INC., NYSE EURONEXT, INC. & BATS GLOBAL MKTS., INC., U.S. MARKET STRUCTURE UPDATE 11 (Apr. 9, 2013), http://www.sec.gov/comments/s7-02-10/s70210-396.pdf. BATS later expressed doubts with respect to the desirability of the trade-at rule. *See* Letter from Eric Swanson, Gen. Counsel & Sec'y, BATS Global Mkts., Inc., to Brent Fields, Sec'y., U.S. Sec. & Exch. Comm'n 4 (Dec. 22, 2014), *available at* http://www.sec.gov/comments/4-657/4657-66.pdf ("BATS believes a trade-at prohibition, which will unquestionably shift the competitive environment in favor of the lit markets, is an intrusive and heavy handed regulatory reaction to concerns that have not been fully analyzed or proven."). On the other hand, NASDAQ recently reiterated its support of a version of the trade-at rule with a reference to the recent regulatory changes in Canada. *See* Letter from Joan C. Conley, Senior Vice President & Corporate Sec'y, to Brent Fields, Sec'y, U.S. Sec. & Exch.

pools and off-exchange market makers precisely because their respective business models often rely on passive matching and de minimis price improvements. These industry players are likely to feel the adverse effect of this regulatory measure, and the model of payment for order flow as such would be considerably strained for securities subjected to the trade-at rule. Indeed, off-exchange market makers openly oppose the trade-at rule, often citing potential wealth transfers, decreased competition, and diminished liquidity,[17] while market makers with no or little off-exchange presence may see this rule "as a critical means to protect displayed liquidity and limit off-exchange passive price matching."[18]

Putting aside the disproportionate effect of the trade-at rule on certain segments of the securities industry, this measure is still a fairly simple and seemingly elegant solution to tackle the problem of fragmentation and the growing share of dark liquidity. The trade-at approach does not require the regulators to pick specific winners and losers among trading venues and business models or to limit the number of execution channels. Interestingly, a recent empirical study of Australia's adoption of the trade-at rule indicates that it has had no adverse impact on liquidity,[19] which lends some support for

---

Comm'n (July 30, 2015), *available at* https://www.sec.gov/comments/265-29/26529-24.pdf.

[17] *See, e.g.*, Letter from John A. McCarthy, Gen. Counsel, KCG Holdings, Inc., to Brent J. Fields, Sec'y, U.S. Sec. & Exch. Comm'n 12 (Dec. 19, 2014), *available at* http://www.sec.gov/comments/4-657/4657-62.pdf (arguing that "the trade-at rule is anticompetitive" and that "[w]holesale market makers . . . provide a valuable service to retail broker-dealers and institutions by handling complex order types . . . that directly compete with exchange offerings").

[18] Letter from Andrew Sevens, Gen. Counsel, IMC Chi. LLC, to Brent Fields, Sec'y, U.S. Sec. & Exch. Comm'n 2–3 (Dec. 30, 2014), *available at* http://www.sec.gov/comments/4-657/4657-89.pdf.

[19] AUSTL. SEC. & INVS. COMM'N, REPORT NO. 394, REVIEW OF RECENT RULE CHANGES AFFECTING DARK LIQUIDITY (May 2014), http://www.asic.gov.au/asic/pdflib.nsf/LookupByFileName/rep394-published-19-May-2014.pdf/$file/rep394-published-19-May-2014.pdf. For some evidence to the contrary, see Sean Foley & Tālis J. Putniņš, Regulatory Efforts to Reduce Dark Trading in Canada and Australia: How Have They Worked? (Oct. 2, 2014) (unpublished manuscript), *available at* http://www.cfainstitute.org/ethics/Documents/Trade-at%20Rule%20Report.pdf.

encouraging the migration of order flow to lit venues.[20] Some variation of the trade-at rule, probably fraught with exceptions, especially for block trading, has a good chance of regulatory approval despite the opposition of several constituencies within the securities industry. As an alternative, several functional equivalents of the trade-at rule—without being labeled as such—could be adopted for the most problematic scenarios. In fact, the trade-at rule is already a part of the tick size pilot jointly pursued by the SEC and the industry, with this pilot applying to a sample of stocks with the market cap of $3 billion or less and the average daily trading volume of a million shares or less.[21] There are already some indications that the SEC is considering a wider scope of the trade-at rule, although its implementation may end up being crude or limited in scope, given the significance of transparency-sensitive trading strategies and the role played by hidden liquidity. Arguably, this rule will have a large market-wide effect if it is in force for very liquid securities rather than just the smaller-cap space. Interestingly, Stephen Luparello, the Director of the SEC's Division of Trading and Markets, suggested that even "a maker-taker pilot with trade-at at the most liquid end of the market" is a possibility.[22]

---

[20] *See also* Daniel Weaver, The Trade-At Rule, Internalization, and Market Quality 1 (Apr. 17, 2014) (unpublished manuscript), *available at* http://ssrn.com/abstract=1846470 (analyzing internalization in U.S. securities markets and concluding that "imposing a trade-at rule on US markets would improve [their] quality").

[21] For the final criteria, as reviewed and revised by the SEC, see Order Approving the National Market System Plan To Implement a Tick Size Pilot Program by Securities Exchanges and FINRA, as Modified by the SEC, for a Two-Year Period, Exchange Act Release No. 74,892, 80 Fed. Reg. 27,514 Exh. A, at 27,548–49 (May 6, 2015), *available at* http://www.gpo.gov/fdsys/pkg/FR-2015-05-13/pdf/2015-11425.pdf.

[22] *Oversight of the SEC's Division of Trading and Markets: Hearing Before the Subcomm. on Capital Mkts. & Gov't Sponsored Enters. of the H. Comm. on Fin. Servs.*, 113th Cong. 28 (2014), *available at* http://www.gpo.gov/fdsys/pkg/CHRG-113hhrg91152/pdf/CHRG-113hhrg91152.pdf (remarks of Stephen Luparello, Director, Division of Trading and Markets, U.S. Securities and Exchange Commission). A recent congressional bill also aims to introduce a maker-taker pilot. Press Release, U.S. Rep. Stephen F. Lynch, Lynch Introduces Legislation to Examine the Risks of the Maker-Taker Pricing Model (Mar. 3, 2015), http://lynch.house.gov/press-release/lynch-introduces-legislation-examine-risks-maker-taker-pricing-model.

H. Impact on Trading Venues and Other Constituencies

The increasing level of fragmentation cannot go on forever, and some regulatory restraints should be expected. Such restraints are likely to be indirect, and, more specifically, some version of the trade-at rule and tweaks to the maker-taker pricing model have a good chance of being adopted. Trading venues would not be the only group to absorb the impact. Some HFT strategies based on inter-venue arbitrage (e.g., market structure arbitrage) are likely to take a hit, and off-exchange market makers would feel an adverse effect caused by lower "touch rates." Likewise, providers of technology and communication solutions might be hurt by restraints on fragmentation that lower demand for their services. If there are fewer trading venues or their geographic dispersion is impacted, the realizable value of such services will also go down.

V. HFT Regulation and Market Structure Reform

Haim Bodek and Stanislav Dolgopolov
Decimus Capital Markets, LLC
October 2015
Adopted from *The Market Structure Crisis in the U.S. Securities Industry in 2015 and Beyond* (a proprietary research report available from Decimus Capital Markets, LLC)

One recurring reaction to various problems of the modern electronic marketplace involves proposals relating to restraints on trading, including specific strategies or techniques, approaches to slowing down or mechanically restraining the trading process, and the elimination of certain shortcuts embedded in the current market structure. A big chunk of proposals can be described as efforts to throw some "sand in the wheels" of HFT and to address the perceived problem of ephemeral liquidity. However, many proposed regulatory measures are nothing more than band-aids in the absence of deeper reforms, such as those aimed at fragmentation. Moreover, as a more effective use of their time, the regulators are already assessing microstructural features that enable questionable trading strategies, particular those related to the practice of latency arbitrage.

Broadly speaking, regulation of HFT does not exist as an autonomous area of securities law, and its de facto reach is centered around recent enforcement actions that highlight the applicability of many facets of regulation to the phenomenon of HFT (e.g., market manipulation, disclosure, market access, systems controls, etc.).[1]

---

[1] The compliance angle is also important. For instance, FINRA developed its own examination guidance for "controls and processes in connection with the development and use of trading algorithms, as well as controls surrounding automated trading technology." *High Frequency Trading*, FINRA (July 2013), http://www.finra.org/industry/high-frequency-trading.

Moreover, there are different definitions of HFT,[2] although this term might be defined with a sufficient degree of specificity in the future legislation / rulemaking. Overall, HFT is likely to be addressed indirectly through incremental / patchwork-like policy changes.

A. Assessing "Sand in the Wheels" Approaches

A wide variety of regulatory proposals and suggestions can be classified as the "sand in the wheels" approach in the sense that they attack the sheer speed- and technology-related factors, such as randomized delays or other speed bumps and frequent batch auctions.[3] Proposals under this umbrella are often framed as anti-HFT or at least as targeting specific predatory forms of HFT. Moreover, such proposals may be adopted through market-wide mandatory rules or emerge through commercial solutions as one dimension of competition, as illustrated by IEX's business model utilizing the famous "magic shoebox" speed bump device.

One obvious target is represented by co-location services offered by trading venues. As an illustration, co-location was attacked by the New York Attorney General in his policy speech,[4] and similar

---

[2] For instance, the SEC's informal definition of HFT as a form of proprietary trading pointed out the following characteristics: "(1) The use of extraordinarily high-speed and sophisticated computer programs for generating, routing, and executing orders; (2) use of co-location services and individual data feeds offered by exchanges and others to minimize network and other types of latencies; (3) very short time-frames for establishing and liquidating positions; (4) the submission of numerous orders that are cancelled shortly after submission; and (5) ending the trading day in as close to a flat position as possible (that is, not carrying significant, unhedged positions over-night)." Concept Release on Equity Market Structure, Exchange Act Release No. 61,358, 75 Fed. Reg. 3594, 3606 (Jan. 14, 2010), *available at* http://www.gpo.gov/fdsys/pkg/FR-2010-01-21/pdf/2010-1045.pdf.

[3] For a package of related proposals pointing in this direction, see John McPartland, *Recommendations for Equitable Allocation of Trades in High-Frequency Trading Environments*, J. TRADING, Spring 2015, at 81.

[4] Eric Schneiderman, N.Y. State Att'y Gen., High-Frequency Trading & Insider Trading 2.0: Remarks Before the New York Law School Panel on "Insider Trading 2.0 – A New Initiative to Crack Down on Predatory Practices" (Mar. 18, 2014), http://www.ag.ny.gov/pdfs/HFT_and_market_structure.pdf.

opinions condemning this feature as such have been heard from different camps. Yet, despite the outcry about the inherent unfairness of co-location, there seems to be little room for regulatory change. Moreover, the SEC itself is focused on nontransparent arrangements related to co-location rather than its very existence. Proximity / co-location advantages have always existed in securities markets, and co-location has many imperfect—and shadier—substitutes. If anything, co-location has been an equalizing force, especially when coupled with "fair access" rules proactively enforced by the regulators and trading venues. As an acceptable and perfectly legal industry practice, this feature is unlikely to disappear, but there will be more scrutiny of fair access, nontransparent preferential arrangements, and tiers of co-location.[5]

Another illustration aimed at creating a "fair access" environment for both professional traders and broader groups of investors is the feature of speed bumps. This feature has been well-publicized in connection with IEX as a commercial solution offered by this investor-friendly trading venue.[6] With regard to the adoption of speed bumps for "leveling the playing field" in securities markets, the most likely scenario is that such devices will be implemented by individual trading venues with no mandatory market-wide rule. At the same time, the adoption of speed bumps by securities exchanges will require explicit approval by the SEC and a careful assessment of their compatibility with the goals of the Securities Exchange Act of 1934 and the core rules of Regulation NMS. While the framework established by Regulation NMS is quite constraining, it is possible that the SEC may balance multiple goals or even grant an exemption

---

[5] For instance, the SEC recently fined the NYSE for providing co-location services without an SEC-vetted rule and attempting to retain disparate fees for pre-existing customers. N.Y. Stock Exch. LLC, Exchange Act Release No. 72,065 (May 1, 2014), http://www.sec.gov/litigation/admin/2014/34-72065.pdf.

[6] Another notable example is PDQ, which employs speed bumps of various lengths for liquidity aggregation, and one of the rationales is to discourage gaming. *See* Ivy Schmerken, *PDQ ATS Launches a New Electronic Equity Auction for Large Orders*, WALL ST. & TECH. (Sept. 22, 2014), http://www.wallstreetandtech.com/trading-technology/pdq-ats-launches-a-new-electronic-equity-auction-for-large-orders-/d/d-id/1315930.

on a case-by-case basis. The regulators are likely to consider new functionalities in light of their anticipated benefits and in the context of harmonization of such functionalities within the National Market System.

The related idea of frequent batch auctions, which could also be randomized, has been viewed favorably by some regulators, industry insiders, and academics.[7] Just like speed bumps, this approach is also being implemented in the real world. One prominent illustration is the Chicago Stock Exchange's initiative to introduce the SNAP feature, which essentially is a randomized frequent batch auction with no order cancellation, and it has been presented as "an innovative solution that *deemphasizes* speed as a hallmark of its functionality, which will operate consistently with Regulation NMS."[8] Yet another related proposal emphasizes applying randomization to aggressive / liquidity-taking orders.[9]

---

[7] Still, the frequent batch auction mechanism was criticized as self-defeating by on the grounds that "liquidity providers' total revenue would decrease because some investors' orders offset each other in each auction [while] the cost associated with adverse selection stays the same because liquidity providers would still absorb the same imbalance of supply and demand." FIA PRINCIPAL TRADERS GRP., UNINTENDED CONSEQUENCES OF FREQUENT BATCH AUCTIONS AS A MARKET DESIGN 3 (2014), *available at* http://www.futuresindustry.org/ptg/downloads/WHITEBOARD%20Frequent%20Batch%20Auctions.pdf.

[8] Notice of Filing of a Proposed Rule Change by Chicago Stock Exchange, Inc. to Implement CHX SNAP℠, an Intra-Day and On-Demand Auction Service, Exchange Act Release No. 75,346, 80 Fed. Reg. 39,172, 39,172 (July 1, 2015), *available at* http://www.gpo.gov/fdsys/pkg/FR-2015-07-08/pdf/2015-16651.pdf. In fact, the SEC approved this proposal, stating that "the SNAP may promote liquidity while minimizing potential information leakage that could disadvantage market participants whose orders are participating in the SNAP Cycle." Order Approving a Proposed Rule Change by Chicago Stock Exchange, Inc. to Adopt and Implement CHX SNAP℠, an Intra-Day and On-Demand Auction Service, Exchange Act Release No. 76,087, 80 Fed. Reg. 61,540 (Oct. 6, 2015), *available at* http://www.gpo.gov/fdsys/pkg/FR-2015-10-13/pdf/2015-25886.pdf.

[9] *See, e.g.*, Letter from Thomas Peterffy, Chairman, Interactive Brokers Grp., to Stephen Luparello, Dir., Div. of Trading & Mkts., U.S. Sec. & Exch. Comm'n (May 8, 2014), *available at* http://www.interactivebrokers.com/download/SEC_proposal_high_frequency_trading.pdf ("We would like to recommend that all U.S. equity and option trading

Another approach, a mandated minimum time period for order exposure, may present a problem because this feature is an option granted to the entire market, and, accordingly, it might be gamed by sophisticated traders.[10] This regulatory measure would be more successful if it is combined with a synchronization of the order submission process, another anti-gaming tool, or some explicit incentive. Interestingly, some trading venues in the United States and Canada, such as NASDAQ OMX PHLX and the Toronto Stock Exchange, have experimented or plan to experiment with minimum exposure order types with special compensation incentives, such as greater liquidity rebates and queue priority,[11] and this approach seems to be more fruitful.

The proposal to establish mandatory cancellation penalties for "excessive" order submission certainly has visible support in the exchange space, with options exchanges (e.g., NYSE Amex Options and NASDAQ OMX PHLX) historically being aggressive experimentators with such penalties. Furthermore, there have been several initiatives by equities exchanges to address this issue. Some of them have made multiple revisions to applicable mechanisms in order to make them workable, as shown by the Chicago Stock Exchange's efforts "to better combat against 'gaming' of the order

---

venues be mandated to hold any order that would remove liquidity for a random period of time lasting between 10 and 200 milliseconds before releasing it to the matching engine.").

[10] *See, e.g.*, SIFMA, IMPACT OF HIGH FREQUENCY TRADING AND CONSIDERATIONS FOR REGULATORY CHANGE 9 (Dec. 13, 2011), *available at* http://www.sifma.org/issues/item.aspx?id=8589936694 ("Although [a minimum quote duration] may seem appropriate for addressing some concerns, such as latency arbitrage, they could be easily gamed. Overall, such requirements would have a negative impact on legitimate trading behavior and thus reduce liquidity and impede legitimate market making activities.").

[11] *See, e.g.*, Order Approving a Proposed Rule Change by NASDAQ OMX PHLX LLC to Introduce the Minimum Life Order as a New Order Type, Exchange Act Release No. 65,926, 76 Fed. Reg. 78,057 (Dec. 9, 2011), *available at* http://www.gpo.gov/fdsys/pkg/FR-2011-12-15/pdf/2011-32141.pdf; Press Release, TMX Grp., TMX Group to Streamline Its Equities Trading Offering (Oct. 23, 2014), http://www.tmx.com/en/news_events/news/news_releases/2014/10-23-2014_TMXGroup-EquitiesTrading.html.

cancellation fee formula."[12] A related regulatory proposal to solve the perceived problem of ephemeral liquidity is to limit the ratio of executed to cancelled orders on a firm-by-firm basis. However, monitoring such ratios *across* trading venues and imposing penalties is also problematic. Overall, anti-cancellation measures have to be carefully tailored to account for real-world features and to avoid interference with legitimate market making. For instance, fragmentation is typically associated with the phenomenon witnessed when liquidity providers submit essentially identical orders across trading venues that are subsequently withdrawn from the market (i.e., cancelled) when the desired quantity is executed. In other words, market making strategies face the conundrum of having to display meaningful quotations across multiple trading venues, resulting in an inflated trading interest that liquidity demanders may incorrectly interpret as intended to be executed in its entirety.

A closely related proposal favors imposing fees for excessive messaging. For instance, such fees could be borne by the most active traders, and a number of strategies relying on rapid quote cancellation could be displaced. This regulatory measure is also tied to the twin issues of infrastructure and bandwidth, and some progress is quite possible. There has been some experimentation with messaging fees by individual trading venues, but these measures were not necessarily successful. Both NASDAQ and Direct Edge introduced excessive messaging penalties,[13] but these specific programs have not been seen as very effective in terms of constraining high-volume participants.

The idea of imposing a transaction tax as a tool to constrain HFT, while implemented in several countries, such as France and Italy,

---

[12] Notice of Filing and Immediate Effectiveness of Proposed Rule Change by Chicago Stock Exchange, Inc. to Amend Its Order Cancellation Fee, Exchange Act Release No. 68,219, 77 Fed. Reg. 69,673, 69,674 (Nov. 20, 2012), *available at* http://www.gpo.gov/fdsys/pkg/FR-2012-11-20/pdf/2012-28135.pdf.

[13] *See* Matt Jarzemsky, *Nasdaq, Direct Edge Move to Tame Quote Traffic*, WALL ST. J. (May 25, 2012), http://online.wsj.com/news/articles/SB10001424052702304840904577426002523828194.

and supported by a group of domestic critics, remains controversial. Most recently, Hillary Clinton as a presidential candidate articulated the need for "a tax targeted specifically at harmful HFT [which] would hit HFT strategies involving excessive levels of order cancellations, which make our markets less stable and less fair,"[14] although this proposal was immediately critiqued on the grounds that high cancellation rates may also be used in market making strategies.[15] Overall, while a general "high-speed" tax is not very likely to be adopted in the United States, a more plausible tax would be tailored to certain opportunistic / harmful / disruptive HFT trading strategies, such as the phenomenon of fleeting liquidity, and tied to meaningful / measurable metrics (e.g., a very short holding period, the absence of market making obligations, a high aggregate cancellation rate, etc.). In any instance, by its very nature, a securities transaction tax will be an obstacle for trading strategies sensitive to transaction costs, and there are numerous empirical studies of such taxes, with many studies being critical of this regulatory tool.[16] Turning to more recent regulatory initiatives with an HFT twist, one empirical study of the recent introduction of a financial transaction tax coupled with a tax on domestic HFT activities in France found "a slight worsening of market quality and a reduction in low-latency activity" and pointed out that "the OTC market has been affected to a much larger degree."[17] A similar study

---

[14] *Hillary Clinton: Wall Street Should Work for Main Street*, HILLARYCLINTON.COM (Oct. 8, 2015), https://www.hillaryclinton.com/p/briefing/factsheets/2015/10/08/wall-street-work-for-main-street/.

[15] *See, e.g.*, Matt Levine, Why Do High-Frequency Traders Cancel So Many Orders?, Bloomberg View (Oct. 8, 2015), http://www.bloombergview.com/articles/2015-10-08/why-do-high-frequency-traders-cancel-so-many-orders-.

[16] *See, e.g.*, CHRISTOPHER L. CULP, COMPASS LEXECON, FINANCIAL TRANSACTION TAXES: BENEFITS AND COSTS (Mar. 16, 2010), *available at* http://www.rmcsinc.com/articles/FTTCLC.pdf.

[17] Jean-Edouard Colliard & Peter Hoffmann, Sand in the Chips? Evidence on Taxing Transactions in Modern Markets 29 (July 31, 2013) (unpublished manuscript), *available at* http://www.rsm.nl/fileadmin/home/Department_of_Finance__VG5_/LQ2013/Jean-Edouard_Colliard_Peter_Hoffmann.pdf.

focusing on Italy found that "there has been an increase in volatility and quoted spreads after the tax introduction."[18]

Overall, while various proposals under the "sand in the wheels" umbrella may be adopted with the growing anti-HFT momentum, there are some problems in terms of generating and implementing specific measures. Moreover, there are serious concerns about meddling with "fast" and "continuous" markets, at least in terms of crafting and implementing mandatory market-wide rules or preventing other forms of gaming. As a result, the regulators are more likely to defer to (or guide) specific regulatory measures by individual trading venues or industry groups.[19] At the same time, the regulators may proceed with selective enforcement and certain forward-looking measures (e.g., modifications to the exceptions under Rule 611) in order to address the most problematic aspects of latency arbitrage.

B. Anti-Disruptive Regulation

Another challenge for proprietary trading is the anti-disruptive rule contemplated by the SEC that would aim at the realities of today's securities markets with their frequent breakdowns. This anti-disruptive rule would reach certain forms of conduct not covered by

---

[18] Tobias R. Rühl & Michael Stein, *The Impact of Financial Transaction Taxes: Evidence from Italy*, 34 ECON. BULL. 25, 32 (2014), *available at* http://www.accessecon.com/Pubs/EB/2014/Volume34/EB-14-V34-I1-P3.pdf.

[19] In fact, Mary Jo White recently described herself as "wary of prescriptive regulation that attempts to identify an optimal trading speed, but . . . receptive to more flexible, competitive solutions that could be adopted by trading venues" and emphasized the following approach: "A key question is whether trading venues have sufficient opportunity and flexibility to innovate successfully with initiatives that seek to de-emphasize speed as a key to trading success in order to further serve the interests of investors. If not, we must reconsider the SEC rules and market practices that stand in the way." Mary Jo White, Chairman, U.S. Sec. & Exch. Comm'n, Enhancing Our Equity Market Structure: Remarks at Sandler O'Neill & Partners, L.P. Global Exchange and Brokerage Conference (June 5, 2014), http://www.sec.gov/News/Speech/Detail/Speech/1370542004312#.U99FBGN5WEc.

the existing antifraud prohibition or other legal tools. More specifically, the envisioned anti-disruptive rule was promised to be "carefully tailored to apply to active proprietary traders in short time periods when liquidity is most vulnerable and the risk of price disruption caused by aggressive short-term trading strategies is highest."[20] This proposal echoes the concern about the Flash Crash of May 6, 2010, as well as subsequent mini-flash crashes and other breakdowns that have plagued the modern electronic marketplace. Such a rule would also join other enacted or contemplated measures aimed at market breakdowns, technological vulnerability, and price volatility (e.g., price bands as a constraint on volatility, systems compliance and integrity measures imposed on trading venues and certain other entities by Regulation SCI, and kill switches as a tool to temporarily disconnect problematic market participants). Depending on how broadly or narrowly this anti-disruptive rule is crafted, a range of trading strategies could be affected. Interestingly, individual trading venues, such as the Chicago Mercantile Exchange, are proceeding with their own versions of anti-disruptive rules—perhaps as a preemptive measure—and there are concerns about such rules' adverse impact on liquidity, which could be read as a large subset of proprietary trading strategies.[21]

C. *Other Structural Restrictions*

There is a handful of proposed structural restrictions that are framed broadly and hence might have a significant impact on securities markets. These measures include constraints on maker-taker arrangements and registration requirements for HFTs. Some of such proposals, such as a lower access fee cap, have favorable odds of

---

[20] *Id.* In addition to any measures that the SEC might take, the CFTC is "currently working on some additional proposals to make sure there are adequate risk controls at all levels, and to minimize the chance that algorithmic trading can cause disruptions or result in unfairness." Chairman Timothy G. Massad, Chairman, U.S. Commodity Futures Trading Comm'n, Keynote Address Before the Beer Institute Annual Meeting (Sept. 9, 2015), http://www.cftc.gov/PressRoom/SpeechesTestimony/opamassad-27.

[21] *See* Mike Kentz, *HFT Crackdown Threatens Liquidity*, INT'L FIN. REV. (Sept. 19, 2014), http://www.ifre.com/hft-crackdown-threatens-liquidity/21164370.article (registration required).

adoption, as well as support of key players in the securities industry. On the other hand, while a reconsideration of Regulation NMS has been prioritized by the SEC and posed to its Equity Market Structure Advisory Committee, a truly comprehensive revision of this pivotal regulation is not as likely. Changes are more likely to be incremental (e.g., revisiting certain components of Regulation NMS, such as the trade-through rule and the ban on locked and crossed markets) or effected via other regulatory norms.

One potential area of reform pertains to maker-taker arrangements. Even a complete abolition of the maker-taker pricing model will not kill HFT, although it would certainly impact the universe of trading strategies and shake out rebate-sensitive firms. One obvious example is rebate arbitrage, which is essentially based on monetizing fee-rebate structures. A more moderate—and realistic— solution is lowering the current cap for access fees mandated by Regulation NMS. This cap, currently set at 0.3 cents per share for equity securities, also functions as a constraint for liquidity rebates. There is some momentum building up in the securities industry, including major market making firms, in favor of this regulatory measure, with the access fee cap potentially knocked down to as low as 0.05 cent per share.[22] This reduction alone would have a great effect on many trading strategies, including controversial high-volume HFT strategies that are effectively subsidized by tiered fee-rebate structures. The impact of a lower access fee cap would narrow the gap between firms that benefit from tiered rebates and fees and firms that do not. Overall, a change in the access fee cap would be a very powerful mechanism for leveling the playing field that the regulators are likely to utilize, if only on a pilot basis. Some securities exchanges are prepared to take (limited) measures in order

---

[22] *See, e.g.*, Letter from Douglas A. Cifu, Chief Exec. Officer, Virtu Fin., to Elizabeth M. Murphy, Sec'y, U.S. Sec. & Exch. Comm'n 2 (Dec. 19, 2014), *available at* http://www.sec.gov/comments/4-657/4657-63.pdf ("[A] reduction in the market access fee cap to a level that is reflective of current market dynamics will ultimately reduce the distortive effect of the maker-taker pricing and simplify our overall fragmented market structure.").

to experiment with lower access fees and liquidity rebates.[23] However, this situation still presents a collective action problem, in which a market-wide change might be more manageable and informative. In fact, the early results of NASDAQ's pilot indicate that this exchange ended up putting itself into a competitive disadvantage,[24] and this outcome shows limitations of unilateral experimentation.

There are numerous calls to subject HFTs to special registration procedures,[25] and this trend may amount to an additional layer of de facto substantive regulation.[26] There are indications that the SEC is seriously considering this course of action.[27] Moreover, some players in the HFT space are not even registered broker-dealers. If future registration requirements include a mandatory broker-dealer status, that would mean a substantial burden in terms of compliance

---

[23] *See, e.g.*, Press Release, Nasdaq, Lowered Access Fees for Key Stocks to Provide Data for Market Structure Improvement (Feb. 2, 2015), http://www.nasdaq.com/press-release/nasdaq-launches-experimental-access-fee-program-20150202-00436.

[24] *See* FRANK HATHEWAY, NASDAQ OMX GRP., INC., NASDAQ ACCESS FEE EXPERIMENT 1–2 (Mar. 2015), http://www.nasdaqomx.com/digitalAssets/97/97754_nasdaq-access-fee-experiment---first-report.pdf.

[25] Such measures would reinforce the existing obligations relating to "large traders." *See* Large Trader Reporting, Exchange Act Release No. 64,976, 76 Fed. Reg. 46,960 (2011) (codified at 17 C.F.R. pts. 240 & 249), *available at* http://www.gpo.gov/fdsys/pkg/FR-2011-08-03/pdf/2011-19419.pdf.

[26] For instance, Richard Ketchum, FINRA's CEO recommended to the SEC "to focus on whether there should be registration requirements for active high-frequency traders." Suzanne Barlyn & Sarah N. Lynch, *Wall Street Regulator Backs Registration for High-Speed Traders*, REUTERS (May 20, 2014), http://www.reuters.com/article/2014/05/20/financial-regulations-highspeedtrading-idUSL1N0O618420140520.

[27] *See* White, Enhancing Our Equity Market Structure, *supra* note. Another related rule proposed by the SEC would require FINRA registration for certain firms, being aimed at "broker-dealers that conduct a significant amount of off-exchange trading activity, including those that engage in so-called high-frequency trading strategies." Exemption for Certain Exchange Members, Exchange Act Release No. 74,581, 80 Fed. Reg. 18,036, 18,043 (proposed Mar. 25, 2015) (to be codified at 17 C.F.R. pt. 240), *available at* http://www.gpo.gov/fdsys/pkg/FR-2015-04-02/pdf/2015-07293.pdf.

and capital requirements. Furthermore, FINRA decided to consider a rule "to establish a registration requirement for associated persons who are: (1) primarily responsible for the design, development or for directing the significant modification of an algorithmic strategy; or (2) responsible for supervising such functions."[28] A more remote possibility is a mandatory scrutiny or vetting of specific algos via external regulatory review. However, this requirement may become an impediment to much-needed modifications of such algos and potentially compromise risk controls. Likewise, it would present tremendous difficulties for the regulators themselves, given their limited resources, unless they just reserve the right of (very) selective inspection and approval.

D. "Plumbing" and the Order Type Controversy

Speed is essential in the low-latency trading arms race, but the relative advantage of this factor alone is diminishing, as cost-effective solutions tailored to the HFT space (e.g., microwave / dark fiber products and FPGA-accelerated market data feeds and order interfaces) have become more readily available in the marketplace. Perhaps a more pivotal advantage covers "plumbing"—meaning the knowledge and use of certain microstructural features in today's securities markets—although regulatory pressure to address asymmetries is this domain is also mounting. Features under the umbrella of plumbing may rely on tiered fees and rebates under the maker-taker pricing model, special order type advantages, fragmentation exploitation (e.g., jockeying for top-of-queue in order to trade or collect a rebate), market structure arbitrage, and de facto side-stepping the ban on locked and crossed markets and the trade-through rule established by Regulation NMS. Overall, the existing regulatory framework, notably Regulation NMS, has been gamed by some HFTs and trading venues by: (i) exploiting regulatory loopholes and clever work-arounds, (ii) exploiting rule contradictions and unintended consequences, (iii) exploiting weakness in regulatory constraints resulting from implementation

---

[28] Press Release, Fin. Indus. Regulatory Auth., FINRA Board Approves Series of Equity Trading and Fixed Income Rulemaking Items (Sept. 19, 2014), http://www.finra.org/Newsroom/NewsReleases/2014/P600831.

and / or latency, (iv) exploiting liberal interpretation of grey areas and / or utilizing exceptions for purposes other than the original intent, (v) exploiting undocumented or unanticipated features, and (vi) exploiting exchange membership status with regard to regulatory liability and eligibility for regulatory exceptions.

One important example of plumbing is the use of certain complex and, more importantly, nontransparent order types. This category of trading strategies frequently brings together a number of techniques, such as those involving rebate capture, low-latency processing, and top-of-queue strategies. While the explosion in the number of order types is, in many ways, a natural adjustment of securities markets to the new fragmented, hypercompetitive, and computerized architecture transformed by Regulation NMS,[29] this diversity has led to additional layers of complexity and informational asymmetry accompanied by nontransparent transfers of wealth. The order type approach to plumbing had been used as an edge on numerous occasions stemming from symbiotic relationships between trading venues and certain preferred market participants. The phenomenon of the "order type controversy" first brought to light by Mr. Bodek in 2012 has exposed the issues posed by complex nontransparent order types that disadvantage broader groups of investors and triggered some efforts to implement incremental reforms within exchange order matching engines.[30]

The defining feature of the order type controversy is the existence of informational asymmetries, as opposed to just disparities in market participants' respective abilities to utilize certain order types

---

[29] Even IEX, which otherwise eschews complex order types, has introduced a rather sophisticated "discretionary peg" order type that is aimed "to provide Subscribers with increased ability to manage the price of their resting orders, while protecting them from being disadvantaged by structural inefficiencies in the dissemination of market information." IEX Trading Alert #2014-022, IEX Announces: Discretionary Peg Functionality and Other Upcoming Deployments (Oct. 6, 2014), http://www.iextrading.com/trading/alerts/2014/022/.

[30] For an extensive discussion of the order type controversy, see HAIM BODEK, THE PROBLEM OF HFT: COLLECTED WRITINGS ON HIGH FREQUENCY TRADING & STOCK MARKET STRUCTURE REFORM (2013), *available at* http://www.amazon.com/gp/product/B00B1UDSS4.

or the overall complexity created by expending order type menus. More specifically, from approximately 2006 to 2014, certain order types developed by exchanges to cater to HFT strategies had undocumented features not adequately disclosed during the SEC's vetting process or in trading venues' technical manuals. Likewise, some de facto order types, such as variations of intermarket sweep orders, had essentially bypassed regulatory review and approval on a few occasions.[31] Furthermore, the actual functioning of certain order types in fact contradicted their formal documentation or violated regulatory norms, such as Regulation NMS itself.[32] The existence of informational asymmetries favoring some traders at the expense of others has manifested itself in several ways. More specifically, there have been instances of selective disclosure by trading venues to preferred market participants,[33] and there is evidence of some trading firms' active participation in the order type

---

[31] *See, e.g.*, Letter from Haim Bodek, Managing Principal, Decimus Capital Mkts., LLC, to the U.S. Sec & Exch. Comm'n 5–6 (Sept. 15, 2014), *available at* https://www.sec.gov/comments/s7-02-10/s70210-420.pdf.

[32] *See, e.g.*, UBS Sec. LLC, Securities Act Release No. 9697, Exchange Act Release No. 74,060, at 6 (Jan. 15, 2015), http://www.sec.gov/litigation/admin/2015/33-9697.pdf ("[T]he PPP order type facilitated the very result that Rule 612 was designed to prevent: it allowed one subscriber to gain execution priority over another in the order queue by offering to pay an economically insignificant sub-penny more per share."); EDGA Exch. Inc., Exchange Act Release No. 74,032, at 3 (Jan. 12, 2015), http://www.sec.gov/litigation/admin/2015/34-74032.pdf ("The displayed pricing sliding process described in the rules did not accurately describe how this functionality of the Exchanges operated. Instead of a single price sliding process as described in their rules, the Exchanges accepted three different price sliding order types, called 'Single Re-Price,' 'Price Adjust,' and 'Hide Not Slide' ('HNS'). These three variations of price sliding were not accurately reflected in the rules filed with, or filed with and approved by, as applicable, the Commission under Section 19(b) of the Exchange Act. . . . [A]lthough the Exchanges provided some information about priority and other characteristics of HNS in technical specifications made available to members, the technical specifications did not contain complete and accurate information regarding the operation of HNS.").

[33] *See, e.g.*, *EDGA*, Exchange Act Release No. 74,032, at 3 ("The Exchanges . . . provide[d] complete and accurate information about HNS to some (but not all) members.").

design process.[34] In the zero-sum game of trading, investors accessing the modern electronic marketplace via "wrong" order types can be disadvantaged by being queue-jumped / losing their priority, having their orders rebooked and repositioned, incurring an access fee instead of collecting a liquidity rebate, becoming subjected to unnecessary intermediation, and bearing the downside of sudden price movements.[35]

The securities industry's continuing cleanup efforts are noticeable, and the regulators deserve a lot of credit for these developments. The early steps included NASDAQ's efforts to clarify and explain its order types' functionalities and to normalize order types across interfaces, BATS' revision of the price sliding functionality and its admission of the existence of certain ambiguities and inaccuracies in prior regulatory filings, and NYSE Arca's elimination of some order types.[36] As an example, NYSE Arca maintained that its package of changes "removes impediments to and perfects a national market system by simplifying functionality and complexity of its order types" and that "investors will not be harmed and in fact would benefit from the removal of complex functionality."[37] A later trend is the phenomenon of comprehensive order type-focused rule filings by equities exchanges, which purport to enhance disclosure and provide more clarity, while often maintaining that no or little

---

[34] *See, e.g.*, *id* at 7 ("Trading Firm A requested that Direct Edge develop an alternative price-sliding functionality that would permit a displayed order that would otherwise lock or cross a protected quotation to "hide" and be ranked and available to execute on Direct Edge's order book at its original locking price, as opposed to being price-slid and ranked at a new price.").

[35] *See* BODEK, THE PROBLEM OF HFT, *supra* note, at 11–12.

[36] *See, e.g.*, Stanislav Dolgopolov, *High-Frequency Trading, Order Types, and the Evolution of the Securities Market Structure: One Whistleblower's Consequences for Securities Regulation*, 2014 U. ILL. J.L. TECH. & POL'Y 145, 152-53, *available at* http://ssrn.com/abstract=2314574

[37] Notice of Filing of a Proposed Rule Change by NYSE Arca, Inc. to Eliminate Certain Order Types, Modifiers and Related References, Exchange Act Release No. 72,591, 79 Fed. Reg. 41,613, 41,616 (July 10, 2014), *available at* http://www.gpo.gov/fdsys/pkg/FR-2014-07-16/pdf/2014-16653.pdf.

substantive change is being proposed.[38] These proposals have consumed hundreds of pages in the *Federal Register*, and *every single exchange* in the equities space has submitted such a package, with some of them submitting subsequent filings with additional clarifications.

On the other hand, some of these order type-related rule filings are problematic, as they look like efforts to obtain the regulators' approval after the fact and with limited disclosure. Moreover, the question is how these rule changes address various order type abuses. For instance, discontinuing a rarely used order type is a cosmetic change, but correcting questionable features of heavily used order types has much more significance. Overall, it is an open question as to how many order types from the arsenal of HFTs will be impacted as opposed to being left alone or just subjected to enhanced disclosure.[39] One controversial development is the SEC's approval of the much-debated order type changes at the New York Stock Exchange and NYSE MKT chiefly relating to the "add

---

[38] *See, e.g.*, Notice of a Proposed Rule Change by NASDAQ Stock Market LLC to Amend and Restate Certain Nasdaq Rules That Govern the Nasdaq Market Center, Exchange Act Release No. 74,558, 80 Fed. Reg. 16,050 (Mar. 20, 2015), *available at* http://www.gpo.gov/fdsys/pkg/FR-2015-03-26/pdf/2015-06891.pdf; Notice of Filing of a Proposed Rule Change by EDGA Exchange, Inc. to Amend Rules 11.6, 11.8, 11.9, 11.10, and 11.11, Exchange Act Release No. 74,435, 80 Fed. Reg. 12,655 (Mar. 4, 2015), *available at* http://www.gpo.gov/fdsys/pkg/FR-2015-03-10/pdf/2015-05482.pdf; Notice of Filing of a Proposed Rule Change by BATS Exchange, Inc. to Amend Rules 11.9, 11.12, and 11.13, Exchange Act Release No. 74, 247, 80 Fed. Reg. 8720 (Feb. 11, 2015), *available at* http://www.gpo.gov/fdsys/pkg/FR-2015-02-18/pdf/2015-03222.pdf.

[39] For instance, Direct Edge is retiring its controversial "Hide Not Slide" feature. *See* Notice of Filing and Immediate Effectiveness of a Proposed Rule Change by EDGX Exchange, Inc. to Rules 11.6, 11.8, 11.9, 11.10 and 11.11 to Align with Similar Rules of the BATS Exchange, Inc., Exchange Act Release No. 75,479, 80 Fed. Reg. 43,810, 43,811 (July 17, 2015), *available at* http://www.gpo.gov/fdsys/pkg/FR-2015-07-23/pdf/2015-18034.pdf; *see also* Notice of Filing and Immediate Effectiveness of a Proposed Rule Change by EDGA Exchange, Inc. to Amend Certain Rules to Adopt or Align System Functionality with That Currently Offered by BATS Exchange, Inc. and BATS Y-Exchange, Inc., Exchange Act Release No. 74,028, 80 Fed. Reg. 2125 (Jan. 9, 2015), *available at* http://www.gpo.gov/fdsys/pkg/FR-2015-01-15/pdf/2015-00531.pdf.

liquidity only" modifier and its usage for intermarket sweep orders.[40] The critics of these changes, including Mr. Bodek, maintained that the provided disclosure was inadequate, the structuring of such intermarket sweep orders was contrary to Regulation NMS, and the likely usage would be beneficial to HFTs at the expense of other market participants.[41]

In their turn, the regulators are focusing on order type practices. In addition to its ongoing broad investigation of equities and options exchanges, the SEC has started addressing certain order practices in its enforcement actions. One of the first steps in this direction was the censure of NYSE Arca for its usage of mid-point passive liquidity orders in contravention of Regulation NMS, as well as its own rulebook.[42] Finally, within a few days in early 2015, the order type controversy left the realm of conspiracy theory, owing to the SEC's two critical enforcement actions against Direct Edge and UBS.[43] Both of these settlements are primarily "order type" actions that momentarily transformed the market structure landscape, demonstrating the regulators' skillful handling of this complex problem. These enforcement actions involved the largest monetary

---

[40] *See* Order Approving Proposed Rule Changes by New York Stock Exchange LLC and NYSE MKT LLC Amending Exchange Rule 13 to Make the Add Liquidity Only Modifier Available for Limit Orders, and Make the Day Time-in-Force Condition and Add Liquidity Only Modifier Available for Intermarket Sweep Orders, Exchange Act Release No. 73,333, 79 Fed. Reg. 62,223 (Oct. 9, 2014), *available at* http://www.gpo.gov/fdsys/pkg/FR-2014-10-16/pdf/2014-24547.pdf.

[41] For this polemic between the exchange and its critics, see *Comments on NYSE Rulemaking: Notice of Filing of Proposed Rule Change Amending Rule 13 to Make the Add Liquidity Only Modifier Available for Additional Limit Orders and Make the Day Time-In-Force Condition Available for Intermarket Sweep Orders [Release No. 34-72548; File No. SR-NYSE-2014-32]*, U.S. SEC. & EXCH. COMM'N, http://www.sec.gov/comments/sr-nyse-2014-32/nyse201432.shtml (last modified Oct. 9, 2014).

[42] N.Y. Stock Exch. LLC, Exchange Act Release No. 72,065 (May 1, 2014), http://www.sec.gov/litigation/admin/2014/34-72065.pdf.

[43] UBS Sec. LLC, Securities Act Release No. 9697, Exchange Act Release No. 74,060 (Jan. 15, 2015), http://www.sec.gov/litigation/admin/2015/33-9697.pdf; EDGA Exch. Inc., Exchange Act Release No. 74,032 (Jan. 12, 2015), http://www.sec.gov/litigation/admin/2015/34-74032.pdf.

fines up to that date against a securities exchange and an ATS, respectively. The stated facts in these settlements expose the existence of improperly disclosed order type features or even undisclosed order types, selective disclosure of information relating to these order types to preferred market participants, which may also be intimately involved during the design stage, and the material significance of such functionalities. Another implication of these enforcement actions is a clear statement that problems with order types go far beyond mere complexity, as they involve instances of wrongful conduct based on informational asymmetry.

At the same time, the SEC seems to remain on the course of deference to order type rulemaking initiatives of securities exchanges, although rejected order types are not unheard of.[44] Perhaps this regulatory agency intends to focus on discrepancies between complex order types' functionalities and the adequacy of disclosure. In other words, the SEC may stay away from micromanaging order type rule filings or taking measures to control complexity in this fashion, while censuring trading venues for inadequate disclosure. As an illustration, the SEC had requested securities exchanges to assess "whether or not [certain] order types are consistent with how they were described to us in the first instance,"[45] which resulted in the comprehensive rule filings described above. Yet, on some occasions, the regulators have also censured improper uses of certain order types by market participants themselves.[46]

---

[44] *See, e.g.*, Order Disapproving a Proposed Rule Change by NASDAQ Stock Market LLC to Establish "Benchmark Orders," Exchange Act Release No. 68,629, 78 Fed. Reg. 3928 (Jan. 11, 2013), *available at* http://www.gpo.gov/fdsys/pkg/FR-2013-01-17/pdf/2013-00871.pdf.

[45] *Oversight of the SEC's Division of Trading and Markets: Hearing Before the Subcomm. on Capital Mkts. & Gov't Sponsored Enters. of the H. Comm. on Fin. Servs.*, 113th Cong. 28 (2014), *available at* http://www.gpo.gov/fdsys/pkg/CHRG-113hhrg91152/pdf/CHRG-113hhrg91152.pdf (remarks of Stephen Luparello, Director, Division of Trading and Markets, U.S. Securities and Exchange Commission).

[46] *See, e.g.*, Latour Trading LLC, Exchange Act Release No. 76,029, at 6 (Sept. 30, 2015), http://www.sec.gov/litigation/admin/2015/34-76029.pdf ("If Latour is using a set of ISOs to display a post-only order, it must comply with the rules

In addition to regulatory scrutiny and private lawsuits (and despite some setbacks), several factors point in the direction of an adequate resolution of the order type controversy. These factors include potential regulatory measures that strike at the very causes of the order type controversy (e.g., a lower cap on access fees and revisions or reinterpretations of Regulation NMS), the intense industry focus on problems caused by fragmentation and concomitant "innovation," consolidation among trading venues, increased levels of disclosure, and, finally, market-based initiatives (e.g., IEX) that use new business models to protect against order type-related informational asymmetries.

E. Outlook for Traders and Other Constituencies

In general, regulatory measures are likely to change the world of proprietary trading and HFT more specifically. Furthermore, some changes will materialize though the regulators' focus on compliance with the existing laws and regulations, such as sponsored access and cybersecurity issues. In addition to proprietary traders, providers of technological and communication solutions may see a downturn. If a microsecond advantage is negated via a speed buffer or a randomized auction, extensive speed-related investments likewise could become meaningless. Overall, different types of HFTs have varying degrees of exposure to regulatory risks, depending on their strategy and specific trading algos. This exposure may relate to violations of the existing regulatory framework—and hence the issue of legal liability—or the viability of individual business models based on plumbing, as well as the ability to make a switch to other business models (e.g., quantitative analysis rather than regulatory arbitrage). Once again, HFT is not going to be regulated out of existence. While many market participants and representatives of other constituencies are vocal about "predatory" tactics associated with HFT, the utility of other HFT activities is frequently recognized.

---

adopted by exchanges under Rule 610 of Reg NMS and send ISOs to remove any equal- or better-priced protected quotations.").

VI. Leveling the Playing Field: Lit and Dark Trading Venues

Haim Bodek and Stanislav Dolgopolov
Decimus Capital Markets, LLC
October 2015
Adopted from *The Market Structure Crisis in the U.S. Securities Industry in 2015 and Beyond* **(a proprietary research report available from** Decimus Capital Markets, LLC**)**

Trading venues are inside the eye of the market structure hurricane. The existing players in this space potentially have a lot to lose, but some of them have a good chance to emerge as winners in different scenarios of the ongoing regulatory shakedown and the securities industry's evolution. Importantly, trading venues as a group have been the SEC's most important target in its enforcement program.[1]

A. Recent Enforcement Developments

Several enforcement actions by the SEC have targeted trading venues—securities exchanges and ATSs alike. Virtually all of these actions were settlements, which limits their precedential weight, but they still expose common weak spots, such as market data distribution holes,[2] leakages of confidential order-related

---

[1] For a recent discussion of the SEC's recent enforcement record, see Bernice Napach, *SEC Enforcement Chief Looks Back Over the Past Year*, THINKADVISOR (Oct. 19, 2015), http://www.thinkadvisor.com/2015/10/19/sec-enforcement-chief-looks-back-over-the-past-yea.

[2] *See, e.g.*, N.Y. Stock Exch. LLC, Exchange Act Release No. 67,857 (Sept. 14, 2012), http://www.sec.gov/litigation/admin/2012/34-67857.pdf.

information,[3] improper functionalities and / or disclosure of certain order types,[4] existence of "trade-throughs,"[5] and weak controls more generally.[6] Monetary fines imposed on trading venues are in fact unprecedented in terms of the sheer size, but the regulators have avoided, with some exceptions, the nuclear option of securities fraud allegations.[7] In the meantime, both the SEC and CFTC are proceeding with additional investigations of trading venues, notably relating to the existence of nontransparent arrangements between trading venues and preferred market participants.[8] Moreover, even state enforcement agencies have joined the game. The explosive lawsuit brought by the New York Attorney General against Barclays in connection with its dark pool[9] may end up being a joint effort with the federal regulators, and this enforcement action is already serving

---

[3] *See, e.g.*, Liquidnet, Inc., Securities Act Release No. 9596, Exchange Act Release No. 72,339 (June 6, 2014), http://www.sec.gov/litigation/admin/2014/33-9596.pdf.

[4] *See, e.g.*, EDGA Exch. Inc., Exchange Act Release No. 74,032 (Jan. 12, 2015), http://www.sec.gov/litigation/admin/2015/34-74032.pdf

[5] *See, e.g.*, NASDAQ Stock Mkt., LLC, Exchange Act Release No. 69,655 (May 29, 2013), http://www.sec.gov/litigation/admin/2013/34-69655.pdf.

[6] *See, e.g.*, EDGX Exch., Inc., Exchange Act Release No. 65,556 (Oct. 13, 2011), http://www.sec.gov/litigation/admin/2011/34-65556.pdf.

[7] For instance, the SEC settlements with Liquidnet, UBS, and ITG referenced Section 17 of the Securities Act of 1933, which is a more restrictive antifraud provision in contrast to Section 10(b) of the Securities Exchange Act of 1934 and Rule 10b-5. *See* ITG Inc., Securities Act Release No. 9887, Exchange Act Release No. 75,672 (Aug. 12, 2015), http://www.sec.gov/litigation/admin/2015/33-9887.pdf; UBS Sec. LLC, Securities Act Release No. 9697, Exchange Act Release No. 74,060 (Jan. 15, 2015), http://www.sec.gov/litigation/admin/2015/33-9697.pdf; Liquidnet, Inc., Securities Act Release No. 9596, Exchange Act Release No. 72,339 (June 6, 2014), http://www.sec.gov/litigation/admin/2014/33-9596.pdf.

[8] *See, e.g.*, Scott Patterson & Jenny Strasburg, *High-Speed Trading Firms Face New U.S. Scrutiny*, WALL ST. J. (Mar. 18, 2014), http://online.wsj.com/news/articles/SB10001424052702303287804579447610625554506.

[9] The lawsuit passed the initial hurdle by not getting dismissed at an early stage. *See* New York v. Barclays Capital Inc., 47 Misc. 3d 862 (N.Y. Sup. Ct. 2015).

as a template for private lawsuits.[10] Overall, the regulators will continue to exert pressure on trading venues through their enforcement and investigations.[11]

B. Regulatory Immunity

The doctrine of regulatory immunity deflects private—but not government—lawsuits from securities exchanges and certain other entities, such as FINRA, in their capacity as self-regulatory organizations for *official* actions in the context of the broad regulatory scheme established by federal securities law. Despite the evolving role of securities exchanges and their transition to the for-profit model, the federal judiciary has maintained a fairly broad interpretation of the scope of SROs' regulatory activities vis-à-vis their activities as private businesses, although there are outlier cases decided by some courts.[12] As an illustration, one decision pointed to the regulatory nature of the authority "to develop, operate, and maintain the Nasdaq Stock Market, to formulate regulatory policies and listing criteria for the Nasdaq Stock Market, and to enforce those policies and rules."[13] This broad interpretation is important, given that product offerings of securities exchanges are typically submitted to the SEC via the formal rulemaking process and fused with their private regulatory regimes. So far, the doctrine of regulatory immunity has held, but it is continually challenged on legal and public policy grounds with frequent references to demutualization of securities exchanges and their transition to for-profit (and sometimes publicly traded) companies. In other words,

---

[10] The class action lawsuit also passed the initial hurdle. *See* Strougo v. Barclays PLC, No. 14-cv-5797 (SAS), 2015 U.S. Dist. LEXIS 54059 (S.D.N.Y. Apr. 24, 2015).

[11] *See, e.g.*, Dave Michaels & Greg Farrell, *Dark Pools Face More Enforcement Actions, SEC Lawyer Says*, BLOOMBERG (Oct. 14, 2014), http://www.bloomberg.com/news/2014-10-14/dark-pools-face-more-enforcement-actions-sec-lawyer-says.html.

[12] Stanislav Dolgopolov, *High-Frequency Trading, Order Types, and the Evolution of the Securities Market Structure: One Whistleblower's Consequences for Securities Regulation*, 2014 U. ILL. J.L. TECH. & POL'Y 145, 161–66, *available at* http://ssrn.com/abstract=2314574.

[13] DL Capital Grp., LLC v. NASDAQ Stock Mkt., Inc., 409 F.3d 93, 95 (2d Cir. 2005).

this limitation on liability and litigation costs remains in place for securities exchanges.

Overall, securities exchanges, given their SRO status, have some advantages compared to other trading venues, such as dark pools, by being protected from some private lawsuits. In the context of regulatory immunity, there is no private right of action even in instances of securities fraud, such as material misrepresentations and omissions. Furthermore, SROs are able to limit liability via their own rules vetted by the SEC. For instance, NASDAQ's Rule 4626(a), subject to certain limitations that include a special compensatory scheme for the Facebook IPO glitch, disclaims liability for "a failure of the Nasdaq Market Center to deliver, display, transmit, execute, compare, submit for clearance and settlement, adjust, retain priority for, or otherwise correctly process an order, Quote/Order, message, or other data entered into, or created by, the Nasdaq Market Center."[14] On the other hand, SROs firmly remain within the reach of the SEC, as contrasted to private litigants, and the regulators have in fact pursued an aggressive enforcement program in the recent past.

The doctrine of regulatory immunity is certainly controversial in light of its scope, coverage of certain activities that constitute fraudulent conduct, and selective availability (e.g., securities exchanges versus ATSs). Perhaps regulatory immunity is the main reason why self-regulation in securities markets is under attack by numerous critics, who often point to technological glitches and other operational failures of securities exchanges.[15] It is possible that this

---

[14] *NASDAQ Stock Market Rules*, NASDAQ OMX GRP., INC., http://nasdaq.cchwallstreet.com (follow "Rule 4000" hyperlink) (last visited Oct. 9, 2015).

[15] *See, e.g., The Role of Regulation in Shaping Equity Market Structure and Electronic Trading: Hearing Before the S. Comm. on Banking, Hous., & Urban Affairs*, 113th Cong. 47 (2015), *available at* http://www.gpo.gov/fdsys/pkg/CHRG-113shrg91300/pdf/CHRG-113shrg91300.pdf (prepared testimony of Kenneth C. Griffin, founder and CEO, Citadel LLC) ("Limiting this immunity would increase the stakes for exchanges in connection with general culpability for operational failures. Facing liability for operational failures would give exchanges very strong financial incentives to invest heavily in steps to prevent or minimize the impact of operational failures.").

doctrine will be revisited on either judicial or legislative level through a revised interpretation / reallocation of the balance between commercial and regulatory activities or an explicit abolition. However, a more likely scenario is that the underlying problems will be addressed by the regulators rather than private litigants, thus leaving this doctrine largely intact.

C. Fraudulent Conduct

A charge of securities fraud against a trading venue is likely to be based on false or misleading disclosure, which may also be tied to undisclosed arrangements with certain preferred traders. The most obvious types of breaches would include selective disclosure of a certain functionality that contradicts the official rules or facilitation of undisclosed and unapproved order flow arrangements. Both securities exchanges and ATSs are already feeling the heat, given the existence of governmental and private lawsuits alleging securities fraud under federal or state law. Another possibility is that trading venues could be aiding and abetting securities fraud without being primary violators themselves, but this type of misconduct would only expose them to governmental but not private lawsuits. A flurry of disclosures by securities exchange purporting to clarify their rules, such as order type-related issues, or by dark pools to put their Form ATS filings / rulebooks in the public domain may as well create an effect not unlike litigation on the back of corporate accounting restatements, although non-SRO trading venues are a more likely target.

D. Ability to Offer Premium Products

Some recent regulatory actions have indeed addressed trading venues' premium products, such as private data feeds and order types, implying that some of them have been used by trading venues to grant inappropriate advantages or are otherwise detrimental to the marketplace. Moreover, there might be additional enforcement actions targeting premium products that are inconsistent or incomplete in regulatory filings and possibly create an informational edge for preferred market participants, although the SEC is still likely to defer to trading venues during the rulemaking stage.

Overall, while many premium products, such as co-location, are likely to survive, less transparent and hence more controversial products may disappear or be subjected to more stringent disclosure. Moreover, there is some degree of competition between trading venues and broker-dealers for certain premium products, such as algorithmic solutions, which is exemplified by the controversy over the "benchmark" order type proposed by NASDAQ but ultimately rejected by the SEC as potentially imposing an undue burden on competition.[16] In this area, trading venues may yield ground or exercise more caution in expanding their product offerings.

E. Rise of Innovative / Anti-Gaming / Investor-Oriented Trading Venues

Despite the crowded trading venue space, there is room for new business models. This phenomenon is exemplified by the rise of IEX, an ATS that plans to acquire the status of a securities exchange. This trading venue emerged as a response to the market structure crisis, and IEX was also a collective protagonist in *Flash Boys*. Not surprisingly, a great deal of support for IEX's model has originated inside the buy-side community. In fact, this trading venue is owned by a group of mutual funds and hedge funds. IEX has implemented a special approach to protect its users from predatory HFT strategies that exploit inter-venue latency differentials. More specifically, IEX employs a 350 microsecond speed bump and thus has time to process price changes before executing orders submitted by low-latency users. Moreover, IEX has invested into getting direct data feeds from all equities exchanges. Yet another feature employed by this trading venue is the broker priority model, which was described by Brad Katsuyama, IEX's CEO, as "our way to say you have the right to internalize for free but you should be doing it out in the

---

[16] Order Disapproving a Proposed Rule Change by NASDAQ Stock Market LLC to Establish "Benchmark Orders," Exchange Act Release No. 68,629, 78 Fed. Reg. 3928, 3929–31 (Jan. 11, 2013), *available at* http://www.gpo.gov/fdsys/pkg/FR-2013-01-17/pdf/2013-00871.pdf.

open."[17] However, after negotiations with the SEC in connection with the bid to become a full-fledged securities exchange, IEX is planning to drop the broker priority model.[18]

In addition to IEX, the space occupied by reform-oriented / buy-side-oriented / anti-HFT / anti-gaming trading venues is becoming populated with a score of existing or potential players marketing themselves as such, including the Chicago Stock Exchange, Sigma X, Knight Match, PDQ, and AQUA. Another notable illustration of an emerging trading venue motivated by concerns about the current market structure is Luminex, a non-profit entity owned by a consortium of institutional investors.[19]

F. Dark Pools

Although there is a natural niche for dark pools when the lack of transparency provides real value (e.g., in terms of price impact), this business model is under attack. Common arguments are that dark liquidity interferes with the process of price discovery. Moreover, there is some skepticism that many dark pools provide much utility for retail orders, as contrasted to block trades, and a related concern is over distortions created by broker-dealer affiliations. In addition to being targeted by governmental agencies, SROs, and private lawsuits, dark pools are also facing industry pressure. For instance, Goldman Sachs was fined by FINRA for violations of the trade-

---

[17] Daniel P. Collins & Jeff Joseph, *Building a Better Market*, FUTURES MAG. (Nov. 1, 2014), http://www.futuresmag.com/2014/11/01/building-a-better-market?t=editors-choice&page=3.

[18] *See* Andrew Ackerman & Bradley Hope, *Trading Platform IEX to Apply for Exchange Status*, WALL ST. J. (July 21, 2015), http://www.wsj.com/articles/trading-platform-iex-to-apply-for-exchange-status-1437510024.

[19] *FAQ*, LUMINEX TRADING & ANALYTICS LLC, http://luminextrading.com/faq.php (last visited Oct. 9, 2015). *See also* John Detrixhe & Sam Mamudi, *Fidelity-BlackRock Group Unveils Dark Pool for Stock Trades*, BLOOMBERG (Jan. 20, 2015), http://www.bloomberg.com/news/2015-01-20/fidelity-blackrock-group-prepares-dark-pool-for-big-stock-trades.html.

through rule in its dark pool, Sigma X,[20] and there had been earlier speculations that this trading venue would be closed down entirely. In fact, several dark pools, such as Pipeline, Wells Fargo Liquidity Crosser, and Vortex, had to close down. Some dark pool sponsors are already repositioning their trading venues "in part to expectations of tighter industry regulations."[21] Yet another signal is the volume drop in the dark pool segment during the period of market turbulence on August 24, 2015, which serves as a proxy for investor confidence.[22]

However, dark pools will survive, especially in the block / large order space, but they will be subjected to a greater level of scrutiny for conflicts of interest, trade-throughs, and the use of delayed data feeds (i.e., the consolidated version rather than private data feeds).[23] Dark pools will be further pressured to engage in self-policing in order to weed out predatory trading done by some HFTs. This self-policing has been marketed to the buy-side by some dark pools, with Barclays facing allegations about misrepresentations in this area, but even more pressure is building up. Another ongoing development is the increasing focus on the level of transparency of dark pools' rulebooks and trading protocols,[24] and, in fact, many dark pools

---

[20] Fin. Indus. Regulatory Auth. & Goldman Sachs Execution & Clearing, L.P., Letter of Acceptance, Waiver and Consent No. 20110307615-01 (June 30, 2014), http://disciplinaryactions.finra.org/viewdocument.aspx?DocNB=36604.

[21] John McCrank, *ConvergEx CEO Says Firm's "Dark Pools" Being Remodeled*, REUTERS (Oct. 10, 2014), http://www.reuters.com/article/2014/10/10/convergex-group-darkpools-idUSL2N0S52XZ20141010.

[22] *See* Sam Mamudi, *Dark Pools Were the Losers as U.S. Markets Saw Volume Spurt*, BLOOMBERG (Aug. 24, 2015), http://www.bloomberg.com/news/articles/2015-08-24/dark-pools-are-the-losers-as-exchanges-get-huge-volume-from-rout.

[23] Interestingly, a recent study suggested that certain dark pools "are slow at obtaining, calculating, and or striking a midpoint price, when, in reality, the fast trader knows that the price is stale," and this factor was interpreted as a "latency tax." Jeff Alexander et al., *Dark Pool Execution Quality: A Quantitative View*, TABB FORUM (Aug. 26, 2015), http://tabbforum.com/opinions/dark-pool-execution-quality-a-quantitative-view (registration required).

[24] *See, e.g.*, Kara M. Stein, Comm'r, U.S. Sec. & Exch. Comm'n, Remarks before the Securities Traders Association's 82nd Annual Market Structure Conference: Market Structure in the 21st Century: Bringing Light to the Dark (Sept. 30, 2015),

have made additional disclosures. Yet, overall, dark pool volumes are likely to decrease substantially due to regulatory pressure and broker liability concerns, as well as investor confidence in dark liquidity more generally. This trend is suggested by the ongoing controversy relating to Barclays' dark pool accompanied by a dropping market share,[25] the explosive settlement concerning ITG's dark pool and a substantial drop in its market share,[26] and some early reports of settlement talks between Credit Suisse, the SEC, and the New York Attorney General in connection with this investment bank's dark pool.[27] Another key factor is the threat of the trade-at rule for off-exchange trading more generally.

---

http://www.sec.gov/news/speech/stein-market-structure.html ("ATSs vary widely in how they approach pricing, order priority, and customers. Against this backdrop, how are investors supposed to evaluate risks and make informed choices? This is why additional transparency is so important to this space."); Annie Massa, *Dark Pools' Governance Rules Also Dark, Says Nasdaq CEO Greifeld*, BLOOMBERG (Oct. 6, 2015), http://www.bloomberg.com/news/articles/2015-10-06/dark-pools-governance-rules-also-dark-says-nasdaq-ceo-greifeld ("The controversy with dark pools right now is not so much the trading per se, but the fact the governance is dark. . . . The customers don't know who's in the dark pool. They don't know what the rules of engagement are.") (quoting Robert Greifeld, CEO of NASDAQ).

[25] *See* Martin Arnold et al., *Banks Start to Drain Barclays Dark Pool*, FIN. TIMES (June 26, 2014), http://www.ft.com/cms/s/0/71268992-fd55-11e3-96a9-00144feab7de.html#axzz3hNKhhI2e;

[26] *See* ITG Inc., Securities Act Release No. 9887, Exchange Act Release No. 75,672 (Aug. 12, 2015), http://www.sec.gov/litigation/admin/2015/33-9887.pdf; Ryan Hoerger et al., *ITG Faces Fight for Reputation Amid Fallout from Dark-Pool Probe*, BLOOMBERG (Aug. 5, 2015), http://www.bloomberg.com/news/articles/2015-08-05/itg-faces-fight-for-reputation-amid-fallout-from-dark-pool-probe; Bradley Hope & Sarah Krouse, *Investigation into Pilot Program Darkens Brokerage's Outlook*, WALL ST. J. (Aug. 6, 2015), http://www.wsj.com/articles/investigation-into-pilot-program-darkens-brokerages-outlook-1438889982. For just one of several private lawsuits related to this controversy, see Complaint, Shah v. Inv. Tech. Grp., Inc., No. 2:15-cv-05921-DSF-FFM (C.D. Cal. Aug. 5, 2015).

[27] Bradley Hope et al., *Credit Suisse Nearing Record Settlement Tied to Wrongdoing at 'Dark Pool'*, WALL ST. J. (Aug. 11, 2015), http://www.wsj.com/articles/credit-suisse-nearing-record-settlement-tied-to-wrongdoing-at-dark-pool-1439315166..

The relationship between dark pools and securities exchanges, although often adversarial, will not be completely antagonistic, given the growing interest of some major exchange groups in the dark liquidity segment. In fact, NASDAQ is planning to take over several dark pools. As asserted by Robert Greifeld, the CEO of NASDAQ OMX Group, "It's apparent to us that a centralized organization running a series of dark pools, while giving independent firms the ability to customize it, can realize tremendous cost savings for them."[28]

G. Trading Venues for Other Asset Classes and Diversification Strategies

One key development for asset classes beyond equities, options, and futures has been the movement away from the over-the-counter model to formal trading platforms, sometimes as a result of an explicit regulatory mandate, such as the Dodd-Frank Act of 2010. This trend may be illustrated by trading platforms for restricted equity securities of pre-IPO / privately held companies and debt instruments. Of course, trading venues like secondary private markets or many debt trading platforms tend to be far removed from the world of HFTs with the focus on highly liquid securities, and the bulk of HFT-style trading strategies simply would not work in that space. On the other hand, this development fits into a diversification strategy for existing players. Broker-dealers and trading venues will continue entering the expanding space for such trading platforms. For instance, NASDAQ is aiming at restricted securities with its Private Market initiative and absorption of SecondMarket, and KCG is targeting the retail bond market with BondPoint. Moreover, KCG's foreign exchange platform, HotSpot QT, was recently sold to BATS. Another illustration is Wake USA, a joint venture between Credit Suisse and Tower Research Capital, an HFT firm, to set up a trading platform for U.S. government securities and other asset classes.

---

[28] Kevin Dugan, *Controversy Isn't Stopping Nasdaq from Taking 'Dark Pool' Plunge*, N.Y. POST (July 23, 2015), http://nypost.com/2015/07/23/controversy-isnt-stopping-nasdaq-from-taking-dark-pool-plunge/.

H. Assessing the Outlook for Trading Venues

Most likely, the blended regulatory regime of governmental and self-regulation will remain in place in spite of attacks on the self-regulatory role of securities exchanges, complaints about uneven regulation of different types of trading venues, and concerns about the for-profit status of the existing SROs. The regulators will not attempt to interfere with the very nature of self-regulation or micromanage different business models, although some privileges enjoyed by SROs might end up being reviewed. On the other hand, trading venues will continue being a target of both government and private lawsuits that potentially include charges of securities fraud. Moreover, the relatively recent transition of securities exchanges to the demutualized for-profit model is unlikely to be reversed despite numerous criticisms of this model, although some trading venues are on the path to remain de facto mutual organizations as a matter of choice, including buy-side-owned entities (e.g., IEX and Luminex). Furthermore, some major securities exchanges and ATSs will continue to be controlled or at least strongly influenced by proprietary trading firms through ownership stakes.

It will be increasingly difficult for trading venues across the dark-lit spectrum to position themselves in a specific niche in order to be attractive to a certain segment of market participants—especially difficult if catering to HFTs—or even survive, given the commercial, regulatory, and legal liability-related pressures stemming from the market structure crisis.[29] This trend may be reinforced in the future by restrictions on the maker-taker pricing model and a greater level of scrutiny of symbiotic relationships between trading venues and preferred traders. Similarly, anti-fragmentation measures, such as the trade-at rule, would also push this space toward consolidation or at least favor securities exchanges at the expense of other trading venues. In the process, some

---

[29] For instance, Citigroup decided to shut down LavaFlow, one of the few remaining ECNs. John McCrank, *Exclusive: Citigroup to Shutter LavaFlow Stock Trading Venue*, REUTERS (Dec. 2, 2014), http://www.reuters.com/article/2014/12/02/us-citigroup-lavaflow-idUSKCN0JG1R520141202.

established / larger players are likely to get a boost at the expense of smaller players or potential entrants. For instance, Jeffrey Sprecher, the CEO of the Intercontinental Exchange, which now owns the NYSE, anticipated that the Big Board would be "a net beneficiary of market structure change."[30] In any instance, more established trading venues will have to continue investing in technology and upgrading their legacy systems in order to maintain their advantages.[31] Moreover, enterprises that provide technology solutions for many market centers, such as NASDAQ OMX Group, are better positioned to monetize technology investments and weather industry downturns via diversified revenue streams.

The process of consolidation will continue in the exchange and dark pool space, as well as among market makers. Some firms will sell off assets to protect their brands as an agency-only franchise, close down units, or simply exit the space altogether. Notable events include the closure of LavaFlow, Pipeline, Apogee, Wells Fargo Liquidity Crosser, Vortex, and the CBOE Stock Exchange. An additional incentive to consolidate business units might be provided when several trading venues are already under the same roof.[32]

---

[30] Jeffrey C. Sprecher, Chairman & Chief Exec. Officer, IntercontinentalExchange, Inc., Remarks at Sandler O'Neill & Partners, L.P. Global Exchange and Brokerage Conference 6 (June 5, 2014), http://ir.theice.com/~/media/Files/I/Ice-IR/events-presentations/transcript/sandleroneill-icetranscript6-2014.pdf.

[31] For a discussion of the NYSE's efforts to speed up its matching engine, see Matthew Leising & Sam Mamudi, *NYSE Owner Said to Buy Algo Technologies to Overhaul Market*, REUTERS (Apr. 16, 2014), http://www.bloomberg.com/news/2014-04-16/nyse-owner-said-to-buy-algo-technologies-to-modernize-exchange.html. *See also Announcing Pillar: Our New Trading Technology Platform*, INTERCONTINENTAL EXCH. (Jan. 29, 2015), https://www.nyse.com/publicdocs/nyse/notifications/trader-update/ArcaEquities/Pillar_Trader_Update_Jan_2015.pdf (announcing "an integrated trading technology platform that [would allow] connect[ing] to all of our equities and options markets using a single specification [and offer] [s]implified, harmonized order types, terminology and messaging across all of [these] markets").

[32] *See, e.g.*, Bradley Hope, *Can the New York Stock Exchange Be Saved?*, WALL ST. J. (Sept. 1, 2014), http://online.wsj.com/articles/can-the-new-york-stock-exchange-be-saved-1409625002 ("Mr. [Jeffrey] Sprecher [the head of the

---

Intercontinental Exchange, which now owns NYSE Euronext] said he wants to pare the former NYSE Euronext company's five remaining stock and options exchanges down to about two.").

VII. Protecting Customers and Achieving Best Execution: Issues for Retail and Institutional Brokers

Haim Bodek and Stanislav Dolgopolov
Decimus Capital Markets, LLC
October 2015
Adopted from *The Market Structure Crisis in the U.S. Securities Industry in 2015 and Beyond* (a proprietary research report available from Decimus Capital Markets, LLC)

The brokerage community has to bear the impact of a variety of market structure-related issues that are currently being addressed by the regulators and tackled by the industry itself through self-regulation and market-based solutions. These issues, often compounded by informational asymmetries and tainted by conflicts of interest, chiefly involve complex functionalities, routing / order handling, payment for order flow arrangements, and fee-rebate structures. More generally, many retail and institutional brokers *and* buy-side institutions, both of which are responsible for execution quality, have fallen behind in terms of their knowledge, competencies, and properly managed exposure to legal risks, although some firms are proactively responding to these challenges.[1] Properly selecting a broker is particularly important in light of the buy-side's oversight responsibilities, including a

---

[1] As an illustration, The Boston Company Asset Management recently teamed up with TABB Metrics to analyze midpoint executions across different dark pool and brokers. *See* Jeff Alexander et al., *Dark Pool Execution Quality: A Quantitative View*, TABB FORUM (Aug. 26, 2015), http://tabbforum.com/opinions/dark-pool-execution-quality-a-quantitative-view (registration required).

fiduciary element. Likewise, retail and institutional brokers are subject to the duty of best execution, which also has a fiduciary element, and they retain that responsibility even if certain order handling / executions tasks are delegated, whether based on a long-term arrangement or otherwise, to an agency broker on a trading venue or an off-exchange market maker.

It would be logical for the market structure crisis to leave a mark on the complex concept of best execution in the context of a highly fragmented marketplace that is often tilted toward HFTs and off-exchange market makers. The duty of best execution stands to absorb the impact of further policy guidance and enforcement, with both of them potentially occurring even in connection with widespread industry practices. Moreover, future policy changes impacting brokers may include additional disclosure requirements and broadly framed reforms of the current market structure, for instance, in connection with certain practices created by the maker-taker pricing model.

A. The Duty of Best Execution

In general, brokers owe to their customers the duty of best execution. While comprised of the sub-duties of care and loyalty, this duty is a multifaceted concept that resists a detailed description or codification. A common misconception even within the brokerage community itself is that executions priced at or within the National Best Bid and Offer necessarily satisfy the duty of best execution. However, a leading precedent had criticized this limited interpretation, while noting that, "[b]ecause the scope of the duty of best execution is constantly evolving . . . broker-dealers have long been required to conform customer order practices with changes in technology and markets."[2] The boundaries of this duty have not been extensively probed in the current market structure, which makes this area a fruitful one for litigation and enforcement. Novel considerations may include a broker's usage of private data feeds and complex order types, broker-affiliated dark pools, and recently

---

[2] Newton v. Merrill, Lynch, Pierce, Fenner & Smith, Inc., 135 F.3d 266, 271-75 (3d Cir. 1998).

introduced incentive programs or allocation mechanisms, such as the maker-taker pricing model, and these considerations are directly related to being competent to protect customers or properly managing conflicts of interest.[3] Another factor is the increasing level of customer involvement in the decision-making process of brokers as their agents. As an illustration, FINRA Rule 5310 allows customers to direct their orders to certain venues. The application of this particular norm became publicized in connection with the emergence of IEX and the refusal of some brokers to send orders to that trading venue.[4] In the near future, the practice of customer order routing instructions, which potentially override a broker's routing preferences, may become more common as a sign of the buy-side taking control over execution quality and addressing conflicts of interest.

B. Joint Review of Allocation Mechanisms

The ongoing probes by the SEC and FINRA, which may have been prompted by the increasingly vocal criticism and recent empirical studies, target maker-taker and payment for order flow practices specifically for distortions of brokers' incentives.[5] An additional layer of regulation *directly imposed* on brokers is a real possibility. For instance, Mary Jo White, the SEC Chairman, mentioned in connection with maker-taker and payment for order flow practices that the regulatory agency is considering "a rule that would enhance

---

[3] For instance, several years ago, one court had observed that a broker "[does not] need to purchase depth-of-book data in order to meet its duty of best execution (which requires it to exercise reasonable diligence to obtain favorable order execution terms for customers)." NetCoalition v. SEC, 615 F.3d 525, 530 n.6 (D.C. Cir. 2010). This summary conclusion might get revisited.

[4] *See* Eamon Javers, *Fidelity, Scottrade Deny Clients HFT Antidote*, CNBC (Apr. 30, 2014), http://www.cnbc.com/id/101628113#.

[5] *See, e.g.*, NAT'L EXAM PROGRAM, U.S. SEC. & EXCH. COMM'N, EXAMINATION PRIORITIES FOR 2015, at 3 (n.d.), *available at* http://www.sec.gov/about/offices/ocie/national-examination-program-priorities-2015.pdf; *Order Routing and Execution Quality of Customer Orders*, FINRA (July 2014), http://www.finra.org/industry/order-routing-and-execution-quality-customer-orders.

order routing disclosures" made by brokers,[6] and this step might prove to be a useful tool to fix the underlying problems. Even more radical attacks have been attempted, with some of them proposing to abolish these two allocation mechanisms altogether, such as the request made by Senator Carl Levin to the SEC.[7] An adoption of such far-reaching measures is not a likely scenario, and, in any instance, it could lead to even more questionable alternatives and nontransparent deals. On the other hand, some foreign regulators have taken a more negative view of payment for order flow as such.[8]

C. Maker-Taker and Order Flow Arrangements

In the context of the maker-taker pricing model, brokers often collect rebates and bear fees instead of passing them onto their customers, and the latter simply pay an all-inclusive brokerage commission. On the other hand, brokerage agreements with a pass-through mechanism, in addition to the brokerage commission itself, are commonly used in the professional trading space (e.g., quantitative hedge funds, proprietary trading firms, and HFTs). In the absence of a pass-through mechanism, it is not difficult to see that brokers have the dual incentive to route liquidity-making orders to trading venues with higher rebates / more favorable tiered pricing

---

[6] Mary Jo White, Chairman, U.S. Sec. & Exch. Comm'n, Enhancing Our Equity Market Structure: Remarks at Sandler O'Neill & Partners, L.P. Global Exchange and Brokerage Conference (June 5, 2014), http://www.sec.gov/News/Speech/Detail/Speech/1370542004312#.U99FBGN5WEc.

[7] *See* Letter from Carl Levin, Chairman, Permanent Subcomm. on Investigations, U.S. Senate, to Mary Jo White, Chairman, U.S. Sec. & Exch. Comm'n 3 (July 9, 2014), *available at* http://levin.senate.gov/download/levin_letter_sec_070914 ("Further study will not change the fact that conflicts of interest are inherent in the maker-taker system and payments for order flow. The SEC should immediately initiate action to eliminate them."). A milder and much more realistic measure originating within the U.S. Congress called for a maker-taker pilot for a limited set of securities. *See* The Maker-Taker Conflict of Interest Reform Act, H.R. 1216, 114th Cong. (2015), *available at* https://www.congress.gov/bill/114th-congress/house-bill/1216/text.

[8] *See, e.g.*, U.K. FIN. CONDUCT AUTH., TR14/13. BEST EXECUTION AND PAYMENT FOR ORDER FLOW (July 2014), *available at* http://www.fca.org.uk/your-fca/documents/thematic-reviews/tr14-13.

structures and, analogously, liquidity-taking orders to trading venues with lower or zero fees. Taking into account relatively high costs of accessing lit markets that often employ the maker-taker pricing model, brokers have the incentive to court liquidity that offsets customer orders as cost-effectively as possible, a practice that may involve conflicts of interest. For example, to enhance monetization of orders, a broker may seek out liquidity providers to act as counterparties inside that broker's dark pool or internalization / crossing facility in exchange for favorable fees / arrangements that are effectively subsidized by customer commissions.

Overall, the incentives associated with the maker-taker pricing model may create a divergence between the interests of brokers and their clients. In fact, one empirical study concluded that several "popular retail brokers appear to route all nonmarketable limit orders to the venue offering the largest rebate [which] is not optimal from the customer's perspective."[9] Ultimately, the study emphasized that "routing decisions based primarily on rebates/fees are inconsistent with best execution."[10] Moreover, even pass-through arrangements may be abused by brokers via arbitrary allocations of benefits to preferred clients or even themselves (e.g., tiered fee-rebate structures).

Another consideration is that brokers can bifurcate order flow by separately optimizing the economics of marketable and non-marketable orders. For example, a broker can sell marketable orders to off-exchange market makers (instead of paying access fees) and route non-marketable orders to trading venues (and collect liquidity rebates). As an illustration, during a recent Senate hearing, an executive of a leading brokerage firm admitted that his firm gets paid for agency orders in one of these two ways in "[n]early every trade."[11] The real problem is not about brokers getting paid either

---

[9] Robert Battalio et al., Can Brokers Have It All? On the Relation Between Make-Take Fees and Limit Order Execution Quality 34 (Mar. 31, 2015) (unpublished manuscript), *available at* http://ssrn.com/abstract=2367462.
[10] *Id.* at 35.
[11] *Conflicts of Interest, Investor Loss of Confidence, and High Speed Trading in U.S. Stock Markets, Hearing Before the Permanent Subcomm. on Investigations*

way—unless these arrangements are not adequately disclosed to customers—but whether either category of orders could have been executed more effectively. This bifurcation has already received attention in one of the lawsuits alleging breaches of the duty of best execution.[12]

An often-floated proposal is to institute a mandatory pass-through of fees and rebates to customers—contrasted to the current practice of such fees and rebates being absorbed / retained by brokers. However, this proposal would be difficult to implement, given the complexity of many fee-rebate structures, including volume-based tiers, and difficulties of ex post allocation. Another thought-provoking question is why such pass-through arrangements have not become dominant as a *contractual* solution. After all, retail investors tend to be "takers" of liquidity, and an all-inclusive brokerage fee, rather than a pass-through, has a lot of appeal to this group for the sake of simplicity. Furthermore, implementing a pass-through mechanism presents a great operational challenge for, and hence eschewed by, many traditional institutional investors, as they would have to allocate net amounts among different funds / subaccounts. On the other hand, pass-through arrangements are offered by brokers to hedge funds, which often have a simpler investment structure, and non-broker-dealer HFTs, which may engage in maker-taker-based trading strategies. A similar suggestion to incorporate fees and rebates into quotations, in addition to the difficulties of implementation for the consolidated and private data feeds, is also questionable because it would open the door to subpenny increments. Furthermore, such a change would be next to meaningless in the absence of a pass-through mechanism, and the resulting interaction of the duty of best execution and the trade-through rule would present a number of problems. With many other fixes being of questionable value, a lower cap on access fees remains

---

of the S. Comm. on Homeland Sec. & Governmental Affairs, 113th Cong. 45 (2014), available at http://www.gpo.gov/fdsys/pkg/CHRG-113shrg89752/pdf/CHRG-113shrg89752.pdf (answer of Steven Quick, Senior Vice President, Trader Group, TD Ameritrade).

[12] *See, e.g.*, Class Action Complaint for Violations of Federal Securities Laws, Klein v. TD Ameritrade Holding Corp., No. 3:14-cv-05738-MAS-LH para. 52, at 17-18 (D.N.J. Sept. 15, 2014).

the most practical option (and perhaps the only option) available to the regulators for *directly* addressing problems posed by the maker-taker pricing model. This approach compresses the economics of undesirable practices, and it may provide more value than less trading strategies being displaced.

D. Use of Special Order Types

A proper order type selection has an impact on several dimensions of the duty of best execution, such as the probability or timeliness of execution and the trading venue selection. As trading venues are cleaning up their order type practices and moving toward greater transparency, this issue becomes important for brokers and adds to their task of monitoring and reassessing the changing landscape for best execution and their own capabilities. As problematic order types associated with HFT are becoming more transparent, the burden shifts to brokers to account for that factor in the context of the duty of best execution.

More specifically, brokers need to be capable of ensuring that their customers are able (i) to access liquidity across lit and dark trading venues in an efficient manner, (ii) to execute aggressive orders when needed to maximize the probability of execution, (iii) to avoid taker fees when unnecessary, (iv) to avoid being rerouted when away markets are stale, and (v) to avoid inferior executions stemming from latency or rebate arbitrage strategies active in the modern electronic marketplace. Oftentimes, complying with this mandate means using advanced order types in their intended usage scenarios and in a correct manner (e.g., with proper modifiers / parameters). Overall, brokers need to take into account practices that have been enabled by HFT-friendly trading venues beginning around the implementation of Regulation NMS in 2007. It becomes a part of the duty of best execution not to access markets in a manner that is ignorant of HFT strategies and exchange order handling / matching engine practices, as well as the pipeline of ongoing clarifications and other changes in this area. While many execution inefficiencies can be avoided by appropriately using intermarket sweep orders and price-sliding order types in scenarios commonly used by HFTs, it is a prudent strategy for any firm trading respectable volumes to gain familiarity with the full range of exchange order types and their intended capabilities.[13]

E. Choosing a Proper Execution Channel

Choosing a proper execution channel has been a key consideration with respect to the duty of best execution: "In fulfilling his duty to obtain the best available price for his customer, a broker is under an obligation to seek out the best available market in which to execute his customer's orders."[14] The market structure crisis has created several novel problems that stem from the problem of fragmentation and the difficulties associated with interacting with liquidity providers that engage in low-latency trading strategies. More specifically, brokers affiliated with dark pools are in the spotlight to demonstrate the adequacy of execution within such trading venues, and order flow arrangements, including payment for order flow deals, also deserve more scrutiny. In addition to conflicts of interest, brokers are on the hook to demonstrate a proper level of care in terms of having taken *reasonable* measures to protect their customers. For instance, a trading venue may be more toxic or slower than its alternatives for certain types of customers. One specific recommendation to the buy-side, which stems from a recent study on suboptimal executions for a major institutional investor in certain "slow" dark pools, is as follows: "Buy-side traders need to measure their execution quality at granular levels to understand how their brokers are routing orders and the effectiveness of their routing and execution strategies. Not all pools are the same and not all algos access pools appropriately."[15]

---

[13] For a detailed discussion of this topic, see HAIM BODEK, THE PROBLEM OF HFT: COLLECTED WRITINGS ON HIGH FREQUENCY TRADING & STOCK MARKET STRUCTURE REFORM (2013), *available at* http://www.amazon.com/gp/product/B00B1UDSS4.

[14] NORMAN S. POSER & JAMES A. FANTO, BROKER-DEALER LAW AND REGULATION § 16.03[B] (4th ed. 2007 & Supp. 2013).

[15] Larry Tabb, *Dark Pool Execution Quality: A Companion Piece – What Does It Mean and Why Should You Care?*, TABB FORUM (Aug. 26, 2015), http://tabbforum.com/opinions/dark-pool-execution-quality-a-companion-piece-what-does-it-mean-and-why-should-you-care (registration required).

As mentioned earlier, it is futile to give a complete description of the duty of best execution, but there are some statements of guidance that list this concept's major dimensions. An important enforcement action, while addressing the pre-HFT era's practices, still provides a good list of broader relevant considerations in its description of the duty of best execution as "the most favorable terms reasonably available under the circumstances, taking into account price, order size, trading characteristics of the security, speed of execution, clearing costs, and the cost and difficulty of executing an order in a particular market, as well as the potential for price improvement."[16] More specific criteria relevant for the current market structure that a broker should consider in venue selection include (i) considering venue toxicity measures based on transaction cost analysis, (ii) assessing the applicable fee-rebate structure in the context of customer execution goals (iii) ensuring that customers share in the economics of venue volume pricing tiers achieved by that broker (e.g., the differential is not "scalped" by the broker itself or another intermediary without appropriate disclosure), (iv) understanding that venue's usage of the consolidated and direct feeds in its order matching engine for pricing and ensuring compliance, (v) identifying "opt-ins" and "opt-outs" in certain order matching functionalities, particularly in connection with potential customer information leakage, (vi) collecting information on types of order flow typically executed on that venue and the channels (i.e., order types or auctions) associated with such order flow, (vii) assessing the impact of the activity of broker-affiliated trading units on that venue, (viii) assessing potential risks associated with venue-specific enforcement actions and ongoing lawsuits and investigations, and (ix) reviewing the full range of order type functionalities available on that venue.

F. Discriminatory Treatment

The long-standing practices of order flow discrimination and segregation of customers based on order flow toxicity raises many conflicts of interest, including disclosure issues (preferencing one

---

[16] Morgan Stanley & Co., Exchange Act Release No. 55,726, at 2 (May 9, 2007), http://www.sec.gov/litigation/admin/2007/34-55726.pdf

class of customers over others), confidentiality (impermissible use of customer information), and, in extreme cases, the use of discrimination to conduct outright violations of the applicable laws and regulation.[17] An area of significant risk exposure is the off-exchange market making business, where apparent conflicts of interest exist between affiliated units (e.g., smart order routers, dark pools, and trading desks). In fact, off-exchange market makers often run such combined business lines, and brokers need to be aware of such conflicts of interest and be prepared to negotiate relevant agreements accordingly. Furthermore, the common practice of brokers using intermediaries to achieve execution goals creates a myriad of potential areas for non-transparent order handling.[18] More generally, various issues of discriminatory treatment in equities markets, including payment for order flow, fee-rebate structures, co-location, and order types, deserve a book-length treatment. Overall, the problems presented by discriminatory treatment are both disclosure-based and compliance-based (e.g., whether such discrimination is permitted at all by the existing laws and regulations in a given scenario).

G. Off-Exchange Market Makers

Although off-exchange market makers often do not have a direct brokerage relationship with ultimate customers, these market

---

[17] *See, e.g.*, ITG Inc. Securities Act Release No. 9887, Exchange Act Release No. 75,672 (Aug. 12, 2015), http://www.sec.gov/litigation/admin/2015/33-9887.pdf; UBS Sec. LLC, Securities Act Release No. 9697, Exchange Act Release No. 74,060 (Jan. 15, 2015), http://www.sec.gov/litigation/admin/2015/33-9697.pdf; Pipeline Trading Sys. LLC, Securities Act Release No. 9271, Exchange Act Release No. 65,609 (Oct. 24, 2011), http://www.sec.gov/litigation/admin/2011/33-9271.pdf.

[18] *See, e.g.*, PRAGMA SEC., MARKET STRUCTURE 2015, at 3 (Mar. 2015), *available at* http://www.pragmatrading.com/sites/default/files/pdf/market_structure_2015_0.pdf ("One prominent algo broker and dark pool operator offers net pricing by executing client orders at a worse price when there's a better price available in its dark pool, and interposing an affiliate who trades as a principal between the two, capturing the difference as a riskless trading profit."). The real issue here is whether such an arrangement has been appropriately disclosed and customer consent has been properly obtained.

makers may in fact discharge agency-related functions in addition to the principal function pursuant to the applicable order handling agreement with a front-end broker.[19] Moreover, off-exchange market makers in their dual agent-principal capacity are likely to be subject to the duty of best execution, which is sometimes explicitly acknowledged,[20] and this standard is likely to be higher than the duty to avoid trade-throughs established by Regulation NMS.[21] Overall,

---

[19] While such agreements are not necessarily in the public domain, one critical illustration of the assumption of agency functions is the agreement between UBS, a leading securities firm, and Charles Schwab, a leading retail broker. *See* EQUITIES ORDER HANDLING AGREEMENT DATED AS OF OCTOBER 29, 2004 BY AND AMONG UBS SECURITIES LLC, SCHWAB CAPITAL MARKETS L.P., CHARLES SCHWAB & CO., INC., AND THE CHARLES SCHWAB CORPORATION, *reproduced in* The Charles Schwab Corp., Quarterly Report (Form 10-Q) Exh. 10.262 (Nov. 8, 2004).

[20] For instance, one agreement from this category explicitly states that the wholesaler in question, as well as the retail broker, are subject to the duty of best execution. EQUITIES AND OPTIONS ORDER HANDLING AGREEMENT DATED AS OF NOVEMBER 29, 2007 BY AND AMONG E*TRADE FINANCIAL CORPORATION, E*TRADE SECURITIES LLC, AND CITADEL DERIVATIVES GROUP LLC, *reproduced in* E*Trade Financial Corp., Annual Report (Form 10-K) Exh. 10.29, at 9–10 (Feb. 28, 2008). More recently, E*trade sold its market making unit, G1 Execution Services, to Susquehanna and then "entered into an order handling agreement whereby it will route 70 percent of its customer equity order flow to G1X over the next five years, subject to best execution standards." E*Trade Financial Corp., Current Report (Form 8-K), at 2 (Feb. 10, 2014). This transaction took place with an investigation in the background, in which FINRA was looking at order routing practices relating to E*trade and G1X. See Nick Baker, *E*Trade Sells Market Making Unit to Susquehanna for $75 Million*, BLOOMBERG (Oct. 23, 2013), http://www.bloomberg.com/news/articles/2013-10-23/e-trade-sells-market-making-unit-to-susquehanna-for-75-million. On a related note, there is additional guidance in FINRA's rulebook: "The duty to provide best execution to customer orders received from other broker-dealers arises only when an order is routed from the broker-dealer to the member for the purpose of order handling and execution." 5310. Best Execution and Interpositioning, FINRA, http://finra.complinet.com/en/display/display_main.html?rbid=2403&element_id=10455 (last visited Oct. 9, 2015).

[21] *See* Regulation NMS, Exchange Act Release No. 51,808, 70 Fed. Reg. 37,496, 37,631 (June 9, 2005) (to be codified at Order Protection Rule, 17 C.F.R. § 240.611(a)), *available at* http://www.gpo.gov/fdsys/pkg/FR-2005-06-29/pdf/05-11802.pdf (establishing that the trade-through rule applies to "trading centers"); *id.* at 37,623 (to be codified at NMS Security Designation and Definitions, 17 C.F.R. § 240.600(b)(78)) (stating that the term "trading center" includes "an

practices of off-exchange market makers and payment for order flow arrangements themselves may expose these players to liability on the basis of the applicable agency functions. For instance, one controversial issue is whether some off-exchange market makers are engaging in arbitrage between the consolidated and direct data feeds in a manner that raises the issue of violations of the duty of best execution—despite probably being acceptable under the trade-through rule and its exceptions.[22]

H. Electronic Trading Risk Controls

Another persistent area of concern for brokers, which will remain important going forward, pertains to SEC regulations governing sponsored access and electronic trading risk controls more generally. This area is important in light of proprietary trading by non-broker-dealers, with some of them being HFTs, and market manipulation carried out through both fully automated / algo-based and point-and click means. Since the adoption of Rule 15c3-5, known as the Market Access Rule, which governs market access for both principal and agency trading,[23] the SEC has enforced compliance with this rule on a number of occasions, including a settlement with a major investment bank for failing "to prevent the

---

exchange market maker, an OTC market maker, or any other broker or dealer that executes orders internally by trading as principal or crossing orders as agent").

[22] *See* RICHARD REPETTO & MIKE ADAMS, SANDLER O'NEILL + PARTNERS, A VIEW OF MARKET STRUCTURE FROM IEX 3 (Apr. 9, 2014), *available at* https://www.thefinancialengineer.net/wp-content/uploads/2014/04/IEX_ViewMarketStructure0414.pdf ("IEX believes the fact that large wholesale market makers are willing to pay for order flow is indicative of the profit these market makers garner from retail customer flow. And when asked about the 90% of price improvement realized on these retail trades the eBrokers 606 reports support, IEX believes that could be from 'stale pricing' from the SIP as well."). A related question is whether certain complex functionalities offered by some off-exchange market makers are accurately disclosed and function as described.

[23] Risk Management Controls for Brokers or Dealers with Market Access, Exchange Act Release No. 63,241, 75 Fed. Reg. 69,792 (Nov. 3, 2010) (codified at Risk Management Controls for Brokers or Dealers with Market Access, 17 C.F.R. § 240.15c3–5), *available at* http://www.gpo.gov/fdsys/pkg/FR-2010-11-15/pdf/2010-28303.pdf.

entry of orders that exceed pre-set aggregate credit thresholds for customers"[24] and a provider of sponsored access for failing "to ensure compliance with applicable regulatory requirements—such as those for preventing naked short sales, wash trades, manipulative layering and money laundering."[25] Importantly, this liability of brokers may be connected with the duty to take reasonable precautions to prevent violations committed by unrelated parties, for instance, in connection with spoofing / layering. The regulators appear to be taking note that such parties are often based abroad and actively seek to utilize the level of liquidity provided by the U.S. securities markets for manipulative activities.

---

[24] Morgan Stanley & Co., Exchange Act Release No. 73,802, at 2 (Dec. 10, 2014), http://www.sec.gov/litigation/admin/2014/34-73802.pdf.

[25] Wedbush Sec. Inc., Exchange Act Release No. 73,652, Investment Advisers Act Release No. 3971, at 2 (Nov. 20, 2014), http://www.sec.gov/litigation/admin/2014/34-73654.pdf.

VIII. Litigation and the Impact of Enforcement: The Market Structure Perspective

Haim Bodek and Stanislav Dolgopolov
Decimus Capital Markets, LLC
October 2015
Adopted from *The Market Structure Crisis in the U.S. Securities Industry in 2015 and Beyond* (a proprietary research report available from Decimus Capital Markets, LLC)

Aside from raging debates about market reform, some changes are likely to come through litigation, notably lawsuits filed by private litigants in their capacity as investors / shareholders / market participants. Indeed, an integral part of the market structure crisis pertains to violations of the existing laws and regulations that may be addressed by private lawsuits, while complementing the regulators' efforts. Certain practices may be targeted (and deterred) by plaintiffs, and heavy monetary burdens may be imposed by courts on certain players. Aside from legal liability, litigation may also influence market reform, even when lawsuits themselves are not successful. Although the term "litigation" includes lawsuits brought by both private parties and government agencies, the regulators, such as the SEC, often rely on settlements. It is important to note that settlements, while often being authoritative and addressing widespread industry practices, do not necessarily have precedential value for future litigation. Interestingly, in its enforcement actions stemming from the market structure crisis, the SEC has largely, but not always, avoided imputing bad motives and the nuclear option of securities fraud. On the other hand, private litigants, such as the City of Providence, and some state regulators, such as the New York Attorney General, have been more aggressive with making wide-sweeping allegations. Moreover, in some instances, the regulators may prefer high-profile enforcement actions as opposed to addressing such practices through the process of rulemaking, given that some practices are already illegal either as a type of fraud or a technical violation of the underlying laws and regulations.

A. Securities Fraud and New (and Older Analogous) Practices

One key feature of the market structure crisis is the reach of legal tools addressing securities fraud to existing practices and certain actors, which is already driving many private lawsuits. The antifraud prohibition under federal securities law—chiefly Section 10(b) of the Securities Exchange Act of 1934 and Rule 10b-5 promulgated by the SEC pursuant to this statutory provision—is quite broad and adoptive,[1] and this tool is well-suited to address a range of practices stemming from the rapid evolution of the modern electronic marketplace. For some practices, there is little difficulty with conceptualizing them as securities fraud. For instance, such older practices as "spoofing" / "layering" and "marking the close"—now adopted to the current market structure—have already been ruled illegal as market manipulation, a form of securities fraud.[2] Likewise,

---

[1] Importantly, in connection with the federal antifraud prohibition, the SEC, as opposed to private litigants, "does not need to prove investor reliance, loss causation, or damages," although it still has to show "a material misrepresentation or a material omission as to which [the defendant] had a duty to speak, or . . . a fraudulent device; with scienter." SEC v. BankCorp, Ltd., 195 F. Supp. 2d 475, 490–91 (S.D.N.Y. 2002).

[2] *See, e.g.*, Athena Capital Research, LLC, Exchange Act Release No. 73,369 (Oct. 16, 2014), http://www.sec.gov/litigation/admin/2014/34-73369.pdf (sanctioning for "marking the close" and noting the use of technology and complex algorithms); Biremis Corp., Exchange Act Release No. 68,456 (Dec. 18, 2012), http://www.sec.gov/litigation/admin/2012/34-68456.pdf (sanctioning for spoofing / layering and noting that certain strategies were designed to take advantage of other market participants' algorithms). One recent case involving spoofing / layering in futures markets in fact has generated a lot of controversy, as the defendant, a lone trader using a modified off-the-shelf trading platform, might have contributed to the Flash Crash. *See* Complaint for Injunctive Relief, Civil Monetary Penalties, and Other Equitable Relief, CFTC v. Nav Sarao Futures Ltd., No. 1:15-cv-03398 (N.D. Ill. Apr. 17, 2015); Criminal Complaint, United

false and misleading disclosure and certain instances of nondisclosure in connection with market structure developments are definitely within the reach of the antifraud prohibition.

In other instances, the application of the antifraud prohibition is more challenging—but still feasible. As an illustration, there are potential approaches to catching HFTs as primary violators in connection with the order type controversy for deliberately using certain order types that violate the underlying documentation (e.g., a functionality contrary to the corresponding SRO rule filing or the relevant technical manual).[3] This approach may draw on recent enforcement actions that attack certain complex order types, including allegations of inaccurate disclosure, and point to selective disclosure by trading venues to preferred market participants.[4]

Other practices are more difficult to place under the umbrella of securities fraud. For instance, certain principal trading strategies based on the maker-taker pricing model, such as rebate arbitrage, have been viewed as having an artificial market impact[5]—and hence as potentially manipulative. However, it is problematic to classify rebate arbitrage as a form of market manipulation. The key consideration is whether the trading strategy in question produces artificial price patterns, however miniscule, as long as they can be

---

States v. Sarao, No. 15-cr-75 (N.D. Ill. Feb. 11, 2015). Moreover, this case has raised many questions about the adequacy of monitoring by the defendant's broker and the Chicago Mercantile Exchange.

[3] Stanislav Dolgopolov, *High-Frequency Trading, Order Types, and the Evolution of the Securities Market Structure: One Whistleblower's Consequences for Securities Regulation*, 2014 U. ILL. J.L. TECH. & POL'Y 145, 154-61, *available at* http://ssrn.com/abstract=2314574.

[4] *See* UBS Sec. LLC, Securities Act Release No. 9697, Exchange Act Release No. 74,060 (Jan. 15, 2015), http://www.sec.gov/litigation/admin/2015/33-9697.pdf; EDGA Exch. Inc., Exchange Act Release No. 74,032 (Jan. 12, 2015), http://www.sec.gov/litigation/admin/2015/34-74032.pdf..

[5] *See, e.g.*, HUW GRONOW, PRINCIPAL GLOBAL EQUITIES, RISE OF THE MACHINES: ON THE EVOLUTION OF HIGH-FREQUENCY TRADING 4 (Oct. 2012) ("[W]hen a strategy looks to earn both the rebate for posting and the rebate for taking, the effect can be to artificially inflate volumes and attract volume triggers to participation-based strategies on arguably a false premise, similar to the momentum ignition strategies.")

profited from, as opposed to an incidental price effect. More generally, in the absence of artificial profit-making price distortions or violations of the applicable trading protocol, it is hard to classify rebate arbitrage as securities fraud as such, either conceptually or doctrinally, even if other market participants are disadvantaged because their transactions have been displaced, crowded out, or outraced.[6]

Another key consideration is the significance of private regulatory regimes provided by trading venues. A mere violation of a rulebook's provision by a trader does not necessarily translate to a remedy for a private litigant by creating a securities fraud claim. On the other hand, several recent appellate decisions point in the direction that a violation of an SRO rule—and many of such rules indeed govern the applicable trading protocol—may form the basis of a securities fraud claim, and the SEC has stated this position in even stronger terms on a number of occasions.[7] This extension of the antifraud prohibition for breaking SRO rules makes even more sense in the context of a broader scheme to disadvantage investors compared to mere violations of convenience that may or may not be ultimately harmful to other market participants. Furthermore, the distinction between an SRO rule and a non-SRO rule (e.g., a dark pool's rulebook) may be immaterial in terms of attaching liability for their violations.

B. "Front-Running," "Stepping Ahead," and "Order Anticipation"

In addition to a widespread discussion of the meaning of the term "rigged markets" in the aftermath of *Flash Boys*, there is a similar focus on the term "front-running," which captures a gamut of advantages utilized by certain market participants and is often analogized to insider trading. In the context of fragmented securities

---

[6] *See* Stanislav Dolgopolov, *The Maker-Taker Pricing Model and Its Impact on the Securities Market Structure: A Can of Worms for Securities Fraud?*, 8 VA. L. & BUS. REV. 231, 250-57 (2014), *available at* http://ssrn.com/abstract=2399821.

[7] *See* Stanislav Dolgopolov, *Providing Liquidity in a High-Frequency World: Trading Obligations and Privileges of Market Makers and a Private Right of Action*, 7 BROOK. J. CORP. FIN. & COM. L. 303, 336-37, 341-42 (2013), *available at* http://ssrn.com/abstract=2032134.

markets, the term "front-running" is often used as a synonym of the term "latency arbitrage." *Flash Boys* and many other sources have used the term "front-running" rather loosely and differently from its established legal definition, which focuses on abuse of customer orders by brokers. For instance, the head of a reform-oriented exchange defined the term "front-running" as follows: "Technological front-running is a predatory High Frequency Trading tactic that leverages speed advantage, resulting from latency differences between different marketplaces, preferential access to data, co-location, faster communication networks, special order types, and internal processing capabilities, to detect, process and act upon information ahead of all slower market participants."[8] In other words, while there are some problematic (and, in some instances, illegal) forms of conduct associated with these advantages, it would be hard to fit them into the established legal definition of "front-running." While some HFT strategies can indeed be described as an opportunistic market making / arbitrage across different trading venues, it is difficult to catch such strategies with existing legal tools without additional allegations. Overall, as far as the mechanics of HFT strategies go, the terms like "front-running" and "technological front-running" may be unfortunate, as they imply an inherently impermissible advantage. On the other hand, the label "stepping ahead" is more consistent with the nature of many HFT strategies that seek to post aggressively at the top-of-queue ahead of trading interest typically representing institutional investors in a manner that seeks to avoid accumulating inventory associated with adverse order flows.[9]

---

[8] Jos Schmitt, Chief Exec. Officer, Aequitas Innovations Inc., Remarks Before the Economic Club of Canada: What Is Wrong with Canada's Capital Markets? 4 (June 2, 2014), http://aequitasinnovations.com/wp-content/uploads/2014/06/Aequitas_Economic_Club_Speech_Final_020614_Updated.pdf.

[9] *See also* HAIM BODEK, THE PROBLEM OF HFT: COLLECTED WRITINGS ON HIGH FREQUENCY TRADING & STOCK MARKET STRUCTURE REFORM 23 (2013), *available at* http://www.amazon.com/gp/product/B00B1UDSS4 ("HFT scalping is predatory in its aim of stepping ahead of institutional order flows. It can be characterized as an opportunistic and discriminatory mimic of traditional market making – where HFT uses opaque advantages, including special order types,

The SEC's leadership has not jumped to endorse this liberal interpretation of "front-running." For instance, during a recent hearing, in which the issue of "front-running" came up, Mary Jo White declined to use the label of "unlawful insider trading" to refer to the scenarios in which one "more quickly react[s] to execution" of other transactions to capitalize on market impact or uses data feeds provided by trading venues.[10] However, the term "front-running" is sometimes used even within the SEC, although typically in the context of market reform rather than alleged violations of the existing laws and regulations. For instance, as recently characterized by one of the Commissioners, "For over a decade, computers have scanned public information and placed orders based on pre-programmed criteria. While front-running used to occur over periods of minutes, hours, or even days, a well-positioned computer may now be able to process information and place orders in just milliseconds."[11] Other commentators emphasized the distinction between "front-running" based on nonpublic information, such as the knowledge of pending customer orders, and "order anticipation" / "liquidity detection" based on public information.[12] Overall, it is very problematic, if not futile, to outlaw such trading strategies and their latest incarnation, "stepping ahead," but some manifestations of this phenomenon may be addressed through regulatory and market-based means, such as speed bumps, oversight of data feed latency, or venue-specific policing for "aggressive" trading.

---

instead of explicit market making privileges – without the market making obligations.").

[10] *Oversight of the SEC's Agenda, Operations and FY 2015 Budget Request: Hearing Before the H. Comm. on Fin. Servs.*, 113th Cong. 13 (2014) (remarks of Mary Jo White, Chairman, U.S. Securities and Exchange Commission), *available at* http://www.gpo.gov/fdsys/pkg/CHRG-113hhrg88537/pdf/CHRG-113hhrg88537.pdf.

[11] Kara M. Stein, Comm'r, U.S. Sec. & Exch. Comm'n, Remarks Before Trader Forum 2014 Equity Trading Summit (Feb. 6, 2014), http://www.sec.gov/News/Speech/Detail/Speech/1370540761194#.VBMbXmMUO4k.

[12] *See, e.g.,* EUREX EXCH., HIGH-FREQUENCY TRADING—A DISCUSSION OF RELEVANT ISSUES 22 (Feb. 2013), *available at* http://www.eurexchange.com/blob/exchange-en/455384/426058/2/data/presentation_hft_media_workshop_chi_nyc_en.pdf.

C. Major Trends in Enforcement as a Guide for Litigation

While private lawsuits are frequently based on preceding enforcement actions, it is important to point out that the regulators, such as the SEC, have a much broader arsenal of legal tools, while the availability of a private right of action is necessarily narrower. For instance, private investors cannot go directly after violations of the bulk of SEC rules (e.g., the trade-through rule of Regulation NMS), but they may base their claims on false and misleading disclosure. In fact, several recent SEC enforcement actions relating to order type practices raise the issue of faulty disclosure to the general public combined with selective disclosure to preferred market participants.[13] Analogously, disclosure of characteristics of premium products provided by trading venues, such as private data feeds, may be deficient, although the existence of disclaimers may invalidate claims.[14] Likewise, order-routing practices that raise concerns about brokers' potential conflicts of interest or their diligence may translate into lawsuits focused on the duty of best execution.[15] Moreover, clear types of market abuse, such as spoofing / layering,[16] may create a valid claim by a private litigant

---

[13] *See* UBS Sec. LLC, Securities Act Release No. 9697, Exchange Act Release No. 74,060 (Jan. 15, 2015), http://www.sec.gov/litigation/admin/2015/33-9697.pdf; EDGA Exch. Inc., Exchange Act Release No. 74,032 (Jan. 12, 2015), http://www.sec.gov/litigation/admin/2015/34-74032.pdf.

[14] *See* Lanier v. BATS Exch., Inc., Nos. 14-cv-3745 (KBF), 14-cv-3865 (KBF), 14-cv-3866 (KBF), 2015 U.S. Dist. LEXIS 55954 (S.D.N.Y. Apr. 28, 2015).

[15] *See* Amended Complaint, New York v. Barclays Capital, Inc., No. 451391/2014 (N.Y. Sup. Ct. Feb. 3, 2015).

[16] *See* Briargate Trading, LLC, Securities Act Release No. 9959, Exchange Act Release No. 76,104 (Oct. 8, 2015), http://www.sec.gov/litigation/admin/2015/33-9959.pdf; Complaint, SEC v. Milrud, No. 2:15-cv-00237-KM-SCM (D.N.J. Jan. 13, 2015); Athena Capital Research, LLC, Exchange Act Release No. 73,369, Investment Advisers Release No. 3950 (Oct. 16, 2014), http://www.sec.gov/litigation/admin/2014/34-73369.pdf; Visionary Trading LLC, Exchange Act Release No. 71,871, Investment Company Act No. 31,007 (Apr. 4, 2014), https://www.sec.gov/litigation/admin/2014/34-71871.pdf. In the context of futures and commodities markets, "spoofing" has been specifically addressed by the Dodd-Frank Act of 2010, and this provision has been tested in court for its lack of vagueness. *See* United States v. Coscia, No. 14-cr-551, 2015 U.S. Dist. LEXIS 50344 (Apr. 16, 2015).

to the extent that such practices amount to market manipulation and harm is demonstrated.[17] Finally, the regulators' level of expertise, monitoring activities, investigative powers, and incentives for whistleblowers explain why many private lawsuits trail behind enforcement actions.

D. Litigation Landscape

Among the lawsuits prompted by the market structure crisis, the one brought on behalf of the City of Providence and similarly situated investors[18] represents the most salient controversy. Although this lawsuit was dismissed in its entirety,[19] the dismissal is being appealed, and at least some of the lawsuit's portions may be resurrected or repackaged in other cases. The initial complaint was submitted by Robbins Geller Rudman & Dowd LLP, a leading plaintiff-side law firm, and, in a somewhat surprising move, Robbins Geller, acting together with Motley Rice LLC and Labaton Sucharow LLP, were certified as co-lead counsel firms on behalf of a group of institutional investors in the consolidated version of four very similar class actions. This case, initially known as the "Flash Boys Lawsuit," went through a number of mutations. For instance, the original complaint targeted several broad groups of defendants—with some of them being unnamed—such as HFT

---

[17] In the area of market abuse, private lawsuits are also possible in the context of futures and commodities markets. *See, e.g.*, Complaint, HTG Capital Partners, LLC v. Doe(s), No. 1:15-cv-02129 (N.D. Ill. Mar. 10, 2015). This particular lawsuit is moving forward with identifying specific defendants. *See* HTG Capital Partners, LLC v. Doe(s), No. 15-cv-02129, 2015 U.S. Dist. LEXIS 126358 (N.D. Ill. Sept. 22, 2015). At the same time, there is no direct private right of action for certain forms of conduct, such as the ban on "spoofing" introduced by the Dodd-Frank Act. As an example, a recent lawsuit against Allston Trading based on this provision was voluntarily withdrawn. *See* Allston Trading LLC's Motion to Dismiss, Mendelson v. Allston Trading, LLC, No. 1:15-cv-04580 (N.D. Ill. July 22, 2015); Complaint at Law, Mendelson v. Allston Trading, LLC, No. 1:15-cv-04580 (N.D. Ill. May 26, 2015).

[18] Complaint for Violation of the Federal Securities Laws, City of Providence, R.I. v. BATS Global Mkts., Inc., No. 1:14-cv-2811 (S.D.N.Y. Apr. 18, 2014).

[19] *In re* Barclays Liquidity Cross & High Frequency Trading Litig., No. 14-MD-2589 (JMF), 2015 U.S. Dist. LEXIS 113323 (S.D.N.Y. Aug. 26, 2015).

firms, securities exchanges, and brokerage firms, but the subsequently amended complaints focused only on the bulk of equities exchanges and Barclays' dark pool.[20] A later lawsuit somewhat filled this void by targeting a large brokerage firm in connection with payment for order flow and maker-taker arrangements.[21]

Other family of class action lawsuits targets private data feeds provided by securities and futures / commodities exchanges in the context of the market data distribution system. One lawsuit aiming at the CME Group and the affiliated Chicago Board of Trade alleges that these entities "held themselves out to the world as providing real-time and bona fide market data, when in reality throughout this same period, Defendants also profited from side agreements with certain HFTs giving these firms the ability to see price data and unexecuted order information before anyone else in the financial world."[22] Another lawsuit—actually a group of lawsuits brought by the same plaintiff in the context of several market data plans adopted by the securities industry—aimed at several securities exchanges for

---

[20] Second Consolidated Amended Complaint for Violation of the Federal Securities Laws, City of Providence, R.I. v. BATS Global Mkts., Inc., No. 1:14-cv-02811-JMF (Nov. 24, 2014); Consolidated Amended Complaint for Violations of the Federal Securities Laws, City of Providence, R.I. v. BATS Global Mkts., Inc., No. 1:14-cv-02811-JMF (Sept. 2, 2014).

[21] Class Action Complaint for Violations of Federal Securities Laws, Klein v. TD Ameritrade Holding Corp., No. 3:14-cv-05738-MAS-LH (D.N.J. Sept. 15, 2014). This case has been transferred to the federal district court in Nebraska, and there are other similar lawsuits under both federal and state law. *See* Zola v. TD Ameritrade, Inc., Nos. 8:14-cv-288, 8:14-cv-289, 8:14-cv-325, 8:14-cv-341 & 8:14-cv-396, 2015 U.S. Dist. LEXIS 24283 (D. Neb. Feb. 26, 2015). Maker-taker arrangements were also prominently featured in a coordinated series of lawsuits against large brokerage firms. The allegations of violations of the duty of best execution were framed under state law, although this approach may be preempted by federal law. *See* Class Action Complaint, Lim v. Charles Schwab & Co., No. 3:15-cv-02074-EDL (N.D. Cal. May 8, 2015); Class Action Complaint, Rayner v. E*Trade Fin. Corp., No. 5:15-cv-01384-RMW (N.D. Cal. Mar. 25, 2015); Class Action Complaint, Lewis v. Scottrade, Inc., 3:14-cv-02926-JLS-BLM (S.D. Cal. Dec. 11, 2014).

[22] Second Amended Class Action Complaint, Braman v. CME Grp., Inc., No. 1:14-cv-02646 para. 9, at 5 (N.D. Ill. July 22, 2014).

"fail[ing] to live up to their promise to provide . . . the market data in a non-discriminatory manner."[23] This group of lawsuits was quickly dismissed, even without resorting to the doctrine of regulatory immunity, on the grounds that the state law claims were preempted by federal regulation or, alternatively, that no valid contractual breaches had been even alleged.[24] This dismissal is currently being appealed.

Contrasted to the lawsuits described above, the complaint of the New York Attorney General targeting Barclays for its dark pool-related activities is narrow-tailored, fact-intensive, and rich on potentially embarrassing quotes from internal communications and meetings.[25] The allegations paint an unsavory image of Barclays in its quest to boost the profile of its dark pool. The allegations include outright falsification of data in marketing materials and relevant reports about HFT activity in the dark pool and its toxicity, misrepresentations of the level of toxicity brought by certain participants, including Barclays Capital Market Making, misrepresentations about order routing, efforts to cater to HFTs despite representations to the contrary made to institutional investors, selective disclosure of such features as the order-routing protocol applicable to Barclays' customers and characteristics of the dark pool's order flow, misrepresentations about market data processing and latency arbitrage, a heavy bias in routing customer orders to the dark pool, which raised the issue of compliance with the duty of best execution, and terminations and resignations of employees opposed to such practices. If these allegations prove to be true, that would be a black eye to the entire dark pool segment of the securities industry. There are indications that even more dark pools are being investigated by the New York Attorney General and the SEC, as well as reports of upcoming enforcement actions against Barclays and Credit Suisse that may end up producing the record

---

[23] Amended Class Action Complaint, Lanier v. BATS Exch., Inc., No. 1:14-cv-03745 para. 2, at 1 (S.D.N.Y. Aug. 15, 2014).
[24] Lanier v. BATS Exch., Inc., Nos. 14-cv-3745 (KBF), 14-cv-3865 (KBF), 14-cv-3866 (KBF), 2015 U.S. Dist. LEXIS 55954 (S.D.N.Y. Apr. 28, 2015).
[25] *See* Amended Complaint, New York v. Barclays Capital, Inc., No. 451391/2014 (N.Y. Sup. Ct. Feb. 3, 2015).

fines imposed on dark pools.[26] Turning back to Barclays, it has been subject to several private lawsuits patterned on the complaint by the New York Attorney General. Interestingly, while one of them has been dismissed as not presenting valid claims,[27] another one was allowed to proceed.[28]

E. *Lessons from the City of Providence Class Action Lawsuit*

Despite its (not yet final) dismissal, the *City of Providence* class action lawsuit still carries a lot of significance going forward in terms of the nature of claims, the extent of immunity of certain players and practices, and the importance of demonstrating wrongful conduct that causes investor harm. The revised complaint focused on nearly every equities exchange and Barclays' dark pool and dropped several categories of defendants from the original filing, thus leaving a void for potential lawsuits against (i) HFT firms, (ii) brokerage firms (including much-exposed giant retail brokers), (iii) options exchanges, and (iv) other ATSs (dark pools and ECNs). The complaint also had some overlaps with the recent group of cases with similar allegations about private data feeds. On the other hand, the *City of Providence* lawsuit was based on federal securities law, while the data feed cases, now also dismissed, were based on state law of contracts and also included options exchanges.

More specifically, the exchanges were alleged to have engaged in manipulative and deceptive conduct, and participated in such conduct by others by

> (i) charging kickback payments to HFT firms in exchange for situating HFT firms' servers in close proximity to the Exchanges' own order matching

---

[26] Christopher M. Matthews & Bradley Hope, *Credit Suisse, Barclays Could Pay up to $150 Million to Settle 'Dark Pool' Claims*, WALL ST. J. (Oct. 22, 2015), http://www.wsj.com/articles/credit-suisse-barclays-could-pay-up-to-150-million-to-settle-dark-pool-claims-1445536853.
[27] *In re* Barclays Liquidity Cross & High Frequency Trading Litig., No. 14-MD-2589 (JMF), 2015 U.S. Dist. LEXIS 113323 (S.D.N.Y. Aug. 26, 2015).
[28] Strougo v. Barclays PLC, No. 14-cv-5797 (SAS), 2015 U.S. Dist. LEXIS 54059 (S.D.N.Y. Apr. 24, 2015).

servers . . . to create informational asymmetries and otherwise rig the market so that HFT firms could profit from access to, and utilization of, material non-public information; (ii) charging kickback payments to HFT firms in exchange for providing enhanced proprietary data feeds that allow HFT firms to receive enriched trading information at faster delivery speeds than the widely available securities information processor . . . feeds; and (iii) designing and implementing new and exceedingly complex order types to attract order flow and fees from HFT firms and make it possible for those firms to pick off of and manipulate investors' trades, to the detriment of Plaintiffs and the Class.[29]

Analogously, Barclays was alleged to have "likewise engaged in similar misconduct in operating its own alternative trading venue for the benefit of HFT and to the detriment of other market participants."[30] While not named as defendants, HFT firms were alleged to have participated in illegal or allegedly illegal activities, "such as electronic front-running, rebate arbitrage, latency arbitrage, spoofing, layering, and contemporaneous trading."[31]

Ultimately, the complaint asserted that all of the defendants had violated the federal antifraud prohibition under Section 10(b) of the Securities Exchange Act of 1934 and Rule 10b-5 and that the securities exchanges had also violated Section 6 of the Securities Exchange Act of 1934, which sets certain requirements for rules to

---

[29] Second Consolidated Amended Complaint for Violation of the Federal Securities Laws, City of Providence, R.I. v. BATS Global Mkts., Inc., No. 1:14-cv-02811-JMF para. 9, at 4-5 (Nov. 24, 2014) (footnote omitted).
[30] *Id.* para. 11, at 5.
[31] *Id.* para. 15, at 7. Other portions of the complaint added the use of "material, nonpublic information," manipulative trading activities, and "quote spamming" to the list. *Id.* para. 3, at 1-2, para. E, at 139. The terms "electronic front-running," "rebate arbitrage," "latency arbitrage" come straight from *Flash Boys*. MICHAEL LEWIS, FLASH BOYS: A WALL STREET REVOLT 172, 219 (2014).

be adopted by securities exchanges.[32] The complaint also requested several *non-monetary* remedies, such as "directing Defendants to ensure that customer bid and offer prices are provided to all investors and trading entities at the same time"; "prohibiting Defendants from providing a financial incentive in the form of rebates or otherwise to HFT and brokerage firms for placing orders and bids on those exchanges"; and "prohibiting Defendants from providing an informational advantage to any HFT firm via paid-for reduced latency services."[33] In other words, the lawsuit demanded to ban private data feeds, market-taker arrangements, and co-location services as such, going far beyond mere cleanup and additional disclosure and amounting to radical structural changes for the securities industry as a whole.

The *City of Providence* complaint had several novel, as well as more established, theories of liability, which had morphed into a fierce battle of legal arguments.[34] For instance, one contentious issue related to a proper classification of the allegedly illegal practices by HFTs, in which distinctions between proprietary and agency trading are important. While the amended complaint dropped HFTs as defendants, many of its theories of liability were still founded on the alleged illegality of certain HFT practices. Furthermore, given that the plaintiffs specifically targeted arrangements implemented by trading venues, it is important to note that many of these arrangements had to go through regulatory filings and SEC approval, although such arrangements did not necessarily function as described. In any instance, securities exchanges, given their SRO status, may hide behind their regulatory immunity in private

---

[32] Second Consolidated Amended Complaint, *City of Providence v. BATS*, paras. 295-308, at 135-39.

[33] *Id.* para. E, at 140.

[34] *See* Barclays' Memorandum in Further Support of Its Motion to Dismiss the Second Consolidated Amended Complaint, City of Providence, R.I. v. BATS Global Mkts., Inc., No. 1:14-cv-02811-JMF (May 8, 2015); Reply Memorandum of Law in Support of the Exchanges' Motion to Dismiss the Second Consolidated Amended Complaint Pursuant to Federal Rules of Civil Procedure 12(b)(1) and 12(b)(6), City of Providence, R.I. v. BATS Global Mkts., Inc., No. 1:14-cv-02811-JMF (May 8, 2015).

lawsuits, as the line between a regulatory regime and "optional" products provided by the SRO in question is blurry.[35] In any instance, the charge that "Defendants' unlawful conduct caused Plaintiffs and Class members to purchase and sell shares at distorted and manipulated prices, and in doing so damaged Plaintiffs and the Class"[36] was challenged on doctrinal and factual grounds.

Given the charge that "Defendants wrongfully engaged in various fraudulent conduct and/or participated in such conduct by others as detailed herein, including electronic front running, latency arbitrage, rebate arbitrage, spoofing, and layering,"[37] one critical issue is whether all of these activities as such constitute securities fraud or fit the doctrinal boundaries. Furthermore, as the defendants asserted, the underlying "claims amount, at most, to no more than non-actionable aiding and abetting"[38] Importantly, there is no private right of action for aiding and abetting securities fraud in this context, and the most recent version of the complaint re-emphasized the defendants' role as primary violators, given the importance of the legal distinction between primary and secondary violations. In other words, even if some of the allegations prove to be correct, that might point to the necessity of SEC enforcement and give an impetus for the regulators to intervene. Furthermore, the availability of a private right of action against securities exchanges in connection with their alleged violations of Section 6 of the Securities Exchange Act of 1934 relating to the requirements for these trading venues' rules appears to be a controversial legal theory.[39]

---

[35] *But see In re* Facebook, Inc., IPO Sec. & Derivatives Litig., 986 F. Supp. 2d 428, 452 n.11 (2013) ("SEC approval of a rule imposing a duty on an SRO is not the sine qua non of SRO immunity; engaging in regulatory conduct is.") (citing Opulent Fund, L.P. v. Nasdaq Stock Mkt., Inc., No. C-07-03683 RMW, 2007 U.S. Dist. LEXIS 79260, at *14 (N.D. Ca. Oct. 12, 2007)).
[36] Second Consolidated Amended Complaint, *City of Providence v. BATS*, para. 296, at 135.
[37] *Id.* para. 297, at 135.
[38] Reply Memorandum of Law in Support of Exchange Defendants' Motion to Dismiss, *City of Providence v. BATS*, at 1.
[39] *Id.* para. A, at 35-37.

One of the pivotal portions of the *City of Providence* complaint focused on the order type controversy. The essence of this controversy was addressed in the following passage: "By failing to include important information about how their order types worked in their regulatory filings, or failing to make the filings altogether, the Exchanges thwarted the SEC rule-making process. In doing so, they deprived the investing public of adequate notice of order types; they deprived the public of an opportunity to comment; and they deprived the SEC of information essential to performing its statutory regulatory function."[40] The complaint asserted that certain order types "were specifically marketed by the Exchanges to sophisticated traders employing abusive HFT strategies and *not* to institutional investors seeking longer terms [sic] investment strategies."[41] The real problem articulated in the complaint is the existence of informational asymmetries, as certain order types "were not adequately documented and/or disclosed to anyone other than Defendants' favored HFT customers and as a result, the majority of investors, even sophisticated investors handling the portfolios of multi-billion dollar pension funds, did not use them."[42] The complaint also singled out intermarket sweep orders, a special category created by Regulation NMS and implemented by individual exchanges, as "hijacked by the Exchanges and subverted (without the requisite SRO rule making) into a device that facilitates rather than prevents fraudulent and manipulative acts and practices."[43] Another important consideration is that the defendants' order type practices have been long investigated by the SEC, resulting in several settlements,[44] and their factual claims may be scrutinized in a different proceeding.

---

[40] Second Consolidated Amended Complaint, *City of Providence v. BATS*, para. 143, at 71.
[41] *Id.* para. 154, at 75.
[42] *Id.* para. 156, at 77.
[43] *Id.* para. 184, at 88.
[44] *See* EDGA Exch. Inc., Exchange Act Release No. 74,032 (Jan. 12, 2015), http://www.sec.gov/litigation/admin/2015/34-74032.pdf; N.Y. Stock Exch. LLC, Exchange Act Release No. 72,065 (May 1, 2014), http://www.sec.gov/litigation/admin/2014/34-72065.pdf..

Another practice attacked by the complaint pertained to the use of material nonpublic information, which is controversial on both factual and doctrinal grounds. At the same time, resale or other leakages of order-related information, which is supposed to be confidential, by trading venues to third parties is a cause for concern, but this issue demands a fact-intensive inquiry. A recent enforcement action brought by the SEC against Liquidnet shows the relevance of this concern.[45]

On August 26, 2015, the federal district court dismissed the *City of Providence* lawsuit, which was bundled with additional state law claims against Barclays, in its entirety,[46] although this decision is being appealed. Overall, the court made the following observation: "Lewis's book may well highlight inequities in the structure of the Nation's financial system and the desirability for, or necessity of, reform. For the most part, however, those questions are not for the courts, but for commentators, private and semi-public entities (including the stock exchanges), and the political branches of government, which . . . have already taken up the issue."[47] The court held that "the Exchanges are absolutely immune from suit based on their creation of complex order types and provision of proprietary data feeds, both of which fall within the scope of the quasi-governmental powers delegated to the Exchanges."[48] This conclusion is not surprising, given the traditionally broad interpretation of the scope of regulatory immunity by the federal courts, and this particular decision also adopted a rather strong standard of "exclusively non-regulatory," which appears to have been borrowed from the defendants' legal brief.[49] On the other hand, the court made the following conclusion: "[I]t is hard to see how the provision of co-location services serves a regulatory function or

---

[45] *See* Liquidnet, Inc., Securities Act Release No. 9596, Exchange Act Release No. 72,339 (June 6, 2014), http://www.sec.gov/litigation/admin/2014/33-9596.pdf.

[46] *In re* Barclays Liquidity Cross & High Frequency Trading Litig., No. 14-MD-2589 (JMF), 2015 U.S. Dist. LEXIS 113323 (S.D.N.Y. Aug. 26, 2015).

[47] *Id.* at *6–7.

[48] *Id.* at *38–39.

[49] *Id.* at *30, 36, 38.

differs from the provision of commercial products and services that courts have held not to be protected by absolute immunity in other cases. . . . The Exchanges, therefore, are not immune from suit based on the provision of co-location services."[50] The distinction between co-location services and complex order types / private data feeds may seem artificial, and, after all, co-location services also have to go through the process of vetting by the SEC. In any instance, this exclusion of co-location from the scope of regulatory immunity may cause securities exchanges substantial problems in the future.

However, the decision did not have to hinge on the issue of regulatory immunity, which was applicable only (and just partially) to the securities exchanges and not Barclays. As asserted by the court, "Even if the Exchanges were not absolutely immune from suit for much of the conduct at issue in these cases, the [complaints] would be subject to dismissal for failure to state a claim."[51] The court engaged in an extensive discussion of other factors leading to the dismissal, such as the scope of market manipulation, investor reliance, the distinction between primary and secondary violators, and the specificity of the plaintiffs' allegations. Some of the points made by the court are open to debate. For instance, the revised complaint did explicitly use the taxonomy of order type-related abuses in terms of their harm to investors and point at deficient disclosure,[52] and this approach may surface in future lawsuits.

---

[50] *Id.* at *31.
[51] *Id.* at 40–41.
[52] *See* Second Consolidated Amended Complaint for Violation of the Federal Securities Laws, City of Providence, R.I. v. BATS Global Mkts., Inc., No. 1:14-cv-02811-JMF paras. 137–40, at 67–69 (Nov. 24, 2014).

IX. Public Comment Letter on Several Order Type-Related Modifications Proposed by the New York Stock Exchange

Haim Bodek
Decimus Capital Markets, LLC
September 2014
Originally submitted to the U.S. Securities and Exchange Commission

Decimus Capital Markets, LLC ("DCM") appreciates this opportunity to comment on recent developments in the so-called "order type controversy." With the mechanisms of special order type handling being the subject of controversy, it is beyond serious question that accommodation of high-frequency trading strategies via these order types is a central issue for our current equity market structure and its ongoing evaluation by the U.S. Securities and Exchange Commission ("SEC"). This controversy, which dates back to at least 2012, focuses on complex order types and exotic modifiers, including "post only" and "hide and light" functionalities and intermarket sweep orders ("ISOs").[1]

---

[1] *See* HAIM BODEK, THE PROBLEM OF HFT: COLLECTED WRITINGS ON HIGH FREQUENCY TRADING & STOCK MARKET STRUCTURE REFORM (2013), *available at* http://www.amazon.com/gp/product/B00B1UDSS4; *see also* Stanislav Dolgopolov, *High-Frequency Trading, Order Types, and the Evolution of the Securities Market Structure: One Whistleblower's Consequences for Securities Regulation*, 2014 U. ILL. J.L. TECH. & POL'Y 145, *available at* http://ssrn.com/abstract=2314574.

The order type controversy goes beyond the sheer complexity created by ever-expanding order type menus and focuses on problems created by specific order types, their inadequate documentation and disclosure,[2] and their interaction with order types traditionally used by the investing public. While a recent proprietary report naively found "no evidence that exchanges or automated proprietary traders have conspired to create 'killer' order types that disadvantage end investors, as some critics have contended,"[3] the increased level of regulatory scrutiny and numerous rule changes filed by different exchanges paint a different picture. In fact, these rule changes and additional disclosure documents often describe their purpose in terms of correcting, clarifying, and simplifying order types and their complex menus. Moreover, these developments often reveal significant disclosure lapses in the past and sometimes involve undisguised admissions of such lapses by securities exchanges.

DCM commends this trend towards greater transparency, but the order type controversy is far from resolved. Our comment letter addresses a recent rule filing by the New York Stock Exchange ("NYSE")[4] as an illustration of securities exchanges' common practice of introducing complex order types in a manner deliberately intended to introduce asymmetries into the marketplace. DCM believes that this rule change proposed by NYSE, if approved as filed, would set an undesirable precedent encouraging both NYSE and other exchanges to continue introducing features that cater to

---

[2] For a discussion of the adequacy of documentation and disclosure, *see* Haim Bodek, *Reigniting the Order Type Debate: Haim Bodek Explains the Real Issues with 'Undocumented' Order Type Features*, TABB FORUM (Aug. 20, 2014), http://tabbforum.com/opinions/reigniting-the-order-type-debate-haim-bodek-explains-the-real-issues-with-%27undocumented%27-order-type-features.

[3] Peter Chapman, *No Order Type Conspiracy, Rosenblatt Study Says*, TRADERS MAG., Aug. 2013, at 8, 8 (quoting the report).

[4] Notice of Filing of Proposed Rule Change by New York Stock Exchange LLC Amending Rule 13 to Make the Add Liquidity Only Modifier Available for Additional Limit Orders and Make the Day Time-In-Force Condition Available for Intermarket Sweep Orders, Exchange Act Release No. 72,548, 79 Fed. Reg. 40,183 (July 7, 2014), *available at* http://www.gpo.gov/fdsys/pkg/FR-2014-07-11/pdf/2014-16191.pdf.

high-frequency traders at the expense of the investing public, while increasing the complexity of securities markets, contrary to the goals of the National Market System. The proposal creates an impression that it might have been designed by someone intimately familiar with high-frequency trading strategies, including those conducted on competing exchanges and enabled by improperly documented and disclosed order types. It is somewhat surprising that this filing, despite its significance and the recent attention paid to order type practices as a part of a nationwide debate on market structure, has attracted little response by experts versed in the matter, judging by the lack of comment letters.[5] DCM believes this is due in part to the complexity of this filing, which provides little color as for the intended utilization of such order types.

The NYSE filing appears to be inconsistent with Section 6(b)(5) of the Securities Exchange Act of 1934 requiring securities exchanges "to remove impediments to and perfect the mechanism of a free and open market and a national market system, and, in general, to protect investors and the public interest; and . . . not . . . permit unfair discrimination between customers, issuers, brokers, or dealers." Furthermore, as described below, some features proposed in the rule filing either do not comply with Regulation NMS or are unlikely to be implemented and / or used in a compliant manner. Moreover, the proposed filing is contrary to much-publicized statements by the leadership of Intercontinental Exchange Group, the parent company of NYSE Euronext, on order types and the maker-taker pricing model. Accordingly, the approval of this filing is likely to escalate the order type controversy, taking into account the mounting evidence on the improper use of certain order types.

Our comment letter focuses on the advantageous features incorporated into the "post-only" functionality (known on NYSE as "add liquidity only" or "ALO") and the use of ISOs well beyond their intended purpose, as proposed by the rule filing. One relevant

---

[5] Note, however, that this rule filing was picked up by the press. *See* Sam Mamudi, *NYSE Order Revamp Seen Worsening Conflicts That Sprecher Decried*, BLOOMBERG (Aug. 7, 2014), http://www.bloomberg.com/news/2014-08-06/nyse-order-revamp-seen-worsening-conflicts-that-sprecher-decried.html.

observation is that these two concerns are not unique to NYSE, as such features currently exist or have existed on other securities exchanges; however, as discussed below, this rule filing might be an outlier.

NYSE attempts to reclassify certain order types as order type "modifiers" or combinations of modifiers. The distinction between "order types" and "modifiers" is subjective, and it should not be used to mask true functionality or provide incomplete disclosure. What might be considered as a distinct "order type" by others (e.g., DAY ISO ALO) is presented by NYSE as a combination of modifiers. However, the whole may be different from the sum of its parts. The inherent properties of such modifiers may contradict each other or interact in a non-transparent and non-intuitive way, thus creating a lot of leeway for NYSE to decide on how such a combination might work or even allowing discretionary adjustments of this functionality from time to time. Accordingly, NYSE should bear the burden of documenting all material properties of such combinations and making appropriate disclosures to all market participants to account for the potential intended *and* "unintended" consequences.

Of primary concern is that NYSE's proposed implementation of the ALO functionality incorporates additional features that are traditionally of interest to high-frequency traders. Moreover, the ALO functionality, which permits traders to avoid executing in scenarios where they would have to pay taker fees, notably differs from the implementation of similar functionalities at other exchanges. The ALO functionality proposed by NYSE permits such orders to forward-tick price-slide in order to gain a superior queue position when a more aggressive price is permissible (e.g., the away market unlocks or a resting order on NYSE is canceled). The logic proposed in the forward-tick price-sliding feature of NYSE's ALO amounts to little more than a reservation feature for queue priority that is not available to traditional orders, which normally incur taker fees in such scenarios. To be clear, the concept of queue priority referred to here is that NYSE's ALO-designated orders would be able to be rebooked at top-of-queue coincident with top-of-book price changes in a manner that cannot be achieved by traditional order types. Thus NYSE's ALO-designated order is not merely an order type to assist in managing maker-taker fees and rebates, but a powerful mechanism for "lighting up" at top-of-queue at an aggressive price on NYSE in a manner that is algorithmically managed by NYSE itself in a low-latency manner. Furthermore, NYSE's ALO functionality offers this queue-priority perk while providing complete assurance that it captures rebates irrespective of price-aggressiveness (a feature that encourages users of the ALO functionality to enter orders with non-bona fide limit prices while they exploit this queue priority perk). This highly advantageous feature would undoubtedly be exploited within rebate arbitrage strategies employed by high-frequency traders.

Needless to say, NYSE's ALO functionality appears primarily designed to provide queue-priority features that advantage ALO-designated orders over traditional orders. Such features should not be embedded in post-only order types, and, in fact, they have gradually been eliminated from major exchanges as a result of the order type controversy.[6] Minimally, if NYSE aims to embed queue priority features in the ALO functionality, the exchange should be obligated to further disclose the major order interactions in which ALO-designated orders would reserve top-of-queue positions over other orders, which are often disadvantaged by paying taker fees in the exact conditions when ALO-designated orders reserve the top-of-queue position. To be clear, the burden should fall on NYSE to show that the ALO functionality does not amount to a discriminatory treatment of other order types in terms of securing a top-of-queue position. Are there cases of traditional limit orders arriving earlier in time being eligible to be booked with a higher priority at the prices for which the ALO functionality can reserve a superior queue position? If so, NYSE's filing should clearly provide examples of all cases by which other order types can compete on a level playing field with the ALO's reservation feature. If not, NYSE should provide further justification on how the introduction of this

---

[6] One notable example is NASDAQ. *See* Equity Technical Update #2012-24, *Automatic Re-Entry of Price Slid Orders via OUCH to Be Introduced August 2, 2012,* NASDAQTRADER.COM (July 13, 2012), http://www.nasdaqtrader.com/TraderNews.aspx?id=ETU2012-24 [hereinafter NASDAQ's Technical Update].

queue-priority reservation feature is warranted given its potential to reduce the execution quality for investors that generally post non-marketable limit orders.

Overall, while the ALO functionality does not appear to provide queue jumping features in relation to similarly priced orders that are "lit" at the same price, which has been permitted by certain order types operating on several securities exchanges,[7] this functionality effectively serves as a queue priority feature offering a de facto reservation for a new price compared to other order types. This fact (or a refutation thereof) should be clearly disclosed by NYSE. Moreover, a natural question is whether this exclusive price reservation feature serves the broader goal of fair and orderly markets.

In stark contrast to NYSE's implementation of the ALO functionality in a manner that embeds queue priority capabilities, NASDAQ took steps in 2012 to neutralize the usage of its Post-Only functionality as a mechanism for providing queue-priority advantages over other order types. For instance, NASDAQ's price-slid orders, including Post-Only-designated orders would "not be guaranteed time priority over other incoming orders at the same price level."[8] Furthermore, NASDAQ adopted the position that "Post-Only orders that are price slid because of NMS interaction and not because of their post-only instruction are eligible for automatic re-entry. Post-Only orders that are slid due to Post-Only restrictions will remain at their slid price."[9] Hence, NASDAQ's Post-Only functionality is prohibited from being ticked-forward into favorable queue positions in precisely the scenarios in which NYSE proposes it will support with its ALO functionality.

As discussed previously, NYSE's ALO functionality is protected against being executed at aggressive prices, a feature that provides order discrimination and encourages non-bona fide orders (*i.e.*,

---

[7] For a discussion of such order types at other exchanges, see BODEK, *supra* note, at 33–37.
[8] NASDAQ's Technical Update, *supra* note.
[9] *Id.*

selling securities with a non-bona fide limit price that is priced at a significant percentage-point through the best bid or offer to ensure that such an order is posted at the most aggressive price). The fact that NYSE proposes to price-slide overly aggressive ALO-designated orders regardless of price-aggressiveness demonstrates an intent by NYSE to encourage the submission of limit prices that do not reflect the true economics of a security, and whose primary function appears to unfairly preference such orders for rebate capture at the most aggressive price permissible. This feature was eliminated on BATS in mid-2012 and most other major exchanges earlier to penalize such orders by subjecting them to taker fees. More specifically, the corresponding BATS filing made the following statement: "The Exchange proposes to modify the functionality of BATS Post Only Orders . . . to permit such orders to remove liquidity from the Exchange's order book . . . if the value of price improvement associated with such execution equals or exceeds the sum of fees charged for such execution and the value of any rebate that would be provided if the order posted to the BATS Book and subsequently provided liquidity."[10]

Finally, in regard to the ALO functionality, NYSE proposes that such orders, when price-slid, should be implemented in a manner that allows a sophisticated trader to detect hidden orders by analyzing price-sliding confirmation messages, thereby contradicting the implicit representation by NYSE that a hidden order is in fact not detectable unless traded. Unlike its counterparts on other exchanges, the ALO functionality is permitted to forward-tick price-slide to establish prices when the hidden order on the contra side is canceled, thereby leaking information on this hidden order. NYSE provides no justification as to why an ALO-designated order should introduce a "loophole" that not only allows sophisticated firms to infer the existence of hidden orders resting on the book, but also provides the underlying non-public information on when such orders are modified or canceled.

---

[10] Notice of Filing and Immediate Effectiveness of a Proposed Rule Change by BATS Exchange, Inc. to Amend BATS Rules Related to the Operation of BATS Post Only Orders and Match Trade Prevention Functionality, Exchange Act Release No. 67,093, 77 Fed. Reg. 33,798, 33,799 (June 1, 2012), *available at* http://www.gpo.gov/fdsys/pkg/FR-2012-06-07/pdf/2012-13765.pdf.

Building upon the significant distortions embedded in NYSE's ALO functionality, NYSE also seeks approval for the DAY ISO ALO, an advanced order type introduced by this filing. This order type, which has several inadequately documented counterparts on other exchanges, raises significant regulatory concerns, including compliance with Regulation NMS, as well as the feasibility of implementing this order type in a manner compliant with Regulation NMS. There are reasons to doubt that the proposed ALO designation for DAY ISOs complies with the requirements of Regulation NMS—or more specifically, the very definition of ISOs.[11] Conceptually, it is unclear how a DAY ISO with the ALO designation can be used to "sweep" a locked market due to its ineligibility to "take" liquidity. This order type / modifier combination *does not* appear to satisfy the "routed to execute" requirement for sub-clause (ii) of the definition when considering the usage to fulfill the requirement to sweep away markets.

The same order type is also likely to be in conflict with Regulation NMS's prohibition of crossed and locked markets.[12] NYSE, with its proposal to accept a DAY ISO ALO at its aggressive limit price when such an order is non-marketable at the exchange, provides an environment that encourages high-frequency traders to post such orders aggressively with conditions likely to actually lock or appear to lock away markets. Such firms benefit from the protection against incurring taker fees and are able to leverage the self-determination properties to construct NBBO off fast data feeds to utilize such orders in a manner contradictory to the use of ISOs envisioned by Regulation NMS. NYSE is required by Regulation NMS to "[p]rohibit its members from engaging in a pattern or practice of displaying quotations that lock or cross any protected quotation in an NMS stock,"[13] but exactly this behavior is encouraged by NYSE's order type because it is designed to be accepted by the exchange at aggressive prices in conditions where high-frequency

---

[11] Regulation NMS, Exchange Act Release No. 51,808, 70 Fed. Reg. 37,496, 37,621-22 (June 9, 2005) (codified at NMS Security Designation and Definitions, 17 C.F.R. § 240.600(b)(30)), *available at* http://www.gpo.gov/fdsys/pkg/FR-2005-06-29/pdf/05-11802.pdf.

[12] *Id.* at 37,631 (codified at Access to Quotations, 17 C.F.R. § 240.610(d)).

[13] *Id.*

traders actually lock or cross away markets or appear to lock or cross away markets, thus defeating the intended purpose of ISOs to "routed to execute" in such conditions. Notwithstanding the potential scenario that NYSE's implementation is a direct violation of Regulation NMS, it is unclear how NYSE could actually implement DAY ISO ALO orders in a manner that ensures NYSE's duty to comply with Regulation NMS in a proactive manner, given that the exchange would have relinquished control over such orders and thus would accept DAY ISO ALO orders that lock or cross away markets that the exchange would normally reject in the course of fulfilling its obligation of prohibiting a pattern or practice of locking or crossing markets.

Importantly, the responsibility for complying with the provision of Regulation NMS requiring NYSE to prohibit a pattern or practice of locking or crossing markets is imposed on NYSE *directly*, but such compliance issues are not adequately addressed in the rule filing. NYSE does not explain how it will fulfill its obligation to comply with Regulation NMS, and particularly Rule 610 – a difficult prospect, given the properties of this order type. Moreover, the proposed rule change would conflict with other NYSE rules adopted pursuant to Regulation NMS and hence make NYSE's rulebook self-contradictory, and NYSE would not be able to fully enforce this pivotal regulation. Similarly, NYSE provides no explanation as to how a member deploying DAY ISO ALO orders would comply with the definition of ISOs and the order protection mandate of Regulation NMS.

Notably, NYSE's filing does not provide information on the purpose of this order type, the segment of the membership being accommodated, and the likely impact on traditional investors. Furthermore, NYSE itself recognized that ISOs on competing exchanges are not fully documented: "The rules of Nasdaq, BATS, BATS-Y, EDGA, and EDGX do not expressly provide that their versions of ISOs can be day, however, nor do their rules prohibit this functionality. In practice, Nasdaq, BATS, BATS-Y EDGA, and

EDGX all accept ISOs with a day time-in-force condition."[14] This observation only strengthens the case for additional disclosure on DAY ISO ALO orders. Moreover, NYSE's filing, while describing NYSE Arca's PNP ISO order type as analogous, is in fact inconsistent with that order type[15] or, even worse, offers evidence of undocumented features on NYSE Arca.

The likely usage of the proposed DAY ISO ALO would encourage individual market participants to needlessly cause violations of Regulation NMS, including Rules 610 and 611, as they jockey for superior queue position, and, in a practical sense, violate the NYSE rules adopted pursuant to Regulation NMS. Importantly, Regulation NMS requires every "trading center, broker, or dealer responsible for the routing of an intermarket sweep order take reasonable steps to establish that such order meets the requirements [of the ISO definition provided by Regulation NMS.]"[16] In general, by using the ISO designation when sending their orders, market participants effectively undertake the obligation to comply with the very definition of ISO and its relevant characteristics. When a DAY ISO ALO is sent at the displayed price on NYSE and then price-slid due to its ALO modifier, its mechanism contradicts the purpose of the ISO designation as attesting to the purpose of sweeping protected quotations, (e.g., "routed to execute against the full displayed size"[17]). Some market participants planning to use this order type

---

[14] Notice of Filing of Proposed Rule Change by New York Stock Exchange LLC Amending Rule 13 to Make the Add Liquidity Only Modifier Available for Additional Limit Orders and Make the Day Time-In-Force Condition Available for Intermarket Sweep Orders, Exchange Act Release No. 72,548, 79 Fed. Reg. 40,183, 40,186 n.13 (July 7, 2014), *available at* http://www.gpo.gov/fdsys/pkg/FR-2014-07-11/pdf/2014-16191.pdf.

[15] *See* NYSE ARCA, INC., ARCADIRECT API SPECIFICATION: VERSION 4.1, at 86 (2012), https://usequities.nyx.com/sites/usequities.nyx.com/files/arcadirectspecversion4_1_4.pdf.

[16] Regulation NMS, 70 Fed. Reg. at 37,632 (codified at Order Protection Rule, 17 C.F.R. § 240.611(c)). In other words, this obligations is directly imposed on both trading venues and market participants.

[17] *Id.* at 37,622 (codified at NMS Security Designation and Definitions, 17 C.F.R. § 240.600(b)(30)(ii)).

may believe that such use is permissible to protect from taking liquidity against hidden orders (which are not protected quotations per Regulation NMS).[18] However, the definition of ISOs requires that displayed orders are swept when the ISO designation is used, a condition which this order type would not comply with and even obstruct. Moreover, this scenario would undoubtedly occur with great frequency, given NYSE's design and typical strategies of high-frequency traders. There is no comparable version of the DAY ISO ALO offered by another exchange that addresses such issues in sufficient detail in order to determine whether its implementation is compliant with Regulation NMS.[19] Needless to say, in the absence of any acceptable standard or norm, it is questionable whether such an order type could be used in any significant scale that would meet the compliance obligations of securities exchanges and market participants with regard to Regulation NMS.

---

[18] For instance, on LavaFlow ECN, which is an alternative trading system, the purpose of its DAY ISO Add Only order is described as "intended for those firms that utilize a fast market data feed and have already swept the market." LavaFlow ECN, Initial Operation Report, Amendment to Initial Operation Report and Cessation of Operations Report for Alternative Trading Systems (Form ATS) Exh. F at 28 (Aug. 5, 2014), *available at* https://www.lavatrading.com/solutions/LavaFlow_Form_ATS.pdf [hereinafter LavaFlow's Form ATS]. This statement implies that this order type is to be used outside of the conditions under which the ISO definition in Regulation NMS is satisfied, i.e., only after the market has been swept and non-simultaneously.

[19] The extent of documentation of this order type on securities exchanges is essentially limited to its revocation as being redundant. More specifically, the Chicago Stock Exchange had revoked its Post Only ISO order type, which is somewhat similar to NYSE's DAY ISO ALO, arguing that "a Post Only ISO is simply a limit order marked Post Only and BBO ISO." Notice of Filing and Immediate Effectiveness of a Proposed Rule Change by Chicago Stock Exchange, Inc. to Consolidate All CHX Order Types, Modifiers, and Related Terms Under One Rule and to Clarify the Basic Requirements of All Orders Sent to the Matching System, Exchange Act Release No. 69,538, 78 Fed. Reg. 28,671, 28,673 (May 8, 2013), *available at* http://www.gpo.gov/fdsys/pkg/FR-2013-05-15/pdf/2013-11453.pdf. Interestingly, LavaFlow ECN has revealed the existence of not only a DAY ISO Add Only order type, but also a *hidden* version of that order type that may internally "lock[]/cross[]" another displayed order." LavaFlow's Form ATS, *supra* note, Exh. F at 19. DCM maintains that regardless of the specificity of the underlying documentation, which should be fully disclosed in the first place, trading venues and their members are not relieved from complying with Rules 610 and 611 of Regulation NMS with respect to ISOs.

To summarize, in most cases, DAY ISO ALOs would not be bona fide orders satisfying the ISO definition. In order to satisfy this definition, such orders would be required to be routed to execute as needed, be routed simultaneously with other bona fide ISOs, and, for practical purposes, comply with the prohibition of a pattern or practice resulting in crossed or locked market. NYSE should demonstrate that such conditions would be satisfied or revise its proposal accordingly.

Rather surprisingly, NYSE's rule filing contradicts the much-touted position of Jeffrey Sprecher, CEO of ICE, who, after acquiring NYSE, argued for the "simplification" of exchanges' order type menus and criticized the connection between certain order types and the maker-taker pricing model. Importantly, the ALO functionality has a direct connection to the maker-taker pricing model because ALO-designated orders are set to execute only if they would collect rebates instead of incurring fees. In fact, Mr. Sprecher made the following statement this May:

> [I]n order to protect market participants for regulatory breaches and while availing themselves of maker-taker rebates, execution venues have further complicated markets by creating order types that play into maker-taker capture such as the well-named "hide don't slide" among others. . . . The New York Stock Exchange has a significant opportunity to offer solutions that rebuild confidence and protect shareholder value. And we believe that we can start by unilaterally reducing the excessive complexity that exists today, such as the proliferation of order types. Therefore, as a first step towards making our markets less complex, we will voluntarily reduce the number of order types at our U.S. equity exchanges. We've identified over one dozen existing order types that we plan to apply to the SEC for rule changes to eliminate. And beyond that, we will continue to

evaluate our other order types to identify those that may not be providing the market with true utility.[20]

In another critique of the status quo, Mr. Sprecher made the following observation:

> At the NYSE, we have as many as 80 different order types, most of which are there to make sure that somebody gets the right rebate or doesn't breach Reg NMS as they're trying to get a rebate, and don't cause a locked market because they're resting in a market with a high rebate, waiting for a trade to happen there, and that'd just added a lot of complexity to the marketplace.[21]

Furthermore, at a recent congressional hearing, NYSE announced a self-imposed "moratorium on any new, or novel, order types that further segment the market" and confirmed its intention of "the elimination of more than a dozen unique order types."[22] While the proposed DAY ISO ALO is not a "unique" order type in NYSE's rulebook, its functionality is novel to NYSE. In fact, the proposed DAY ISO ALO belongs to the category of the most advanced order types in the arsenal of high-frequency traders, and, traditionally, this category of order types has lacked transparency.

In conclusion, NYSE's filing not only seeks to maintain the status quo, but to return to a time prior to 2012, when little attention was

---

[20] IntercontinentalExchange Grp., Inc., Q1 2014 Earnings Call 10 (May 8, 2014), http://ir.theice.com/files/doc_events/2014/1Q14_transcript.pdf (remarks of Jeffrey C. Sprecher, Chairman & Chief Executive Officer, IntercontinentalExchange Group, Inc.).

[21] Jeffrey C. Sprecher, Chairman & CEO, IntercontinentalExchange, Remarks at the 15th Annual Credit Suisse Financial Services Forum 7 (Feb. 12, 2014), http://ir.theice.com/files/doc_events/2014/CSFB%20Transcript%202-2014.pdf.

[22] *Conflicts of Interest, Investor Loss of Confidence, and High Speed Trading in U.S. Stock Markets, Hearing Before the Permanent Subcomm. on Investigations of the S. Comm. on Homeland Sec. & Governmental Affairs*, 113th Cong. 78 (2014), *available at* http://www.gpo.gov/fdsys/pkg/CHRG-113shrg89752/pdf/CHRG-113shrg89752.pdf (prepared statement of Thomas W. Farley, President, New York Stock Exchange).

paid to the harmful impact of order handling of advanced order types on investors. NYSE's filing introduces features that NASDAQ and BATS neutralized in 2012 amidst regulatory scrutiny. NYSE should provide clear and compelling evidence that its proposal would benefit securities markets and the investing public. NYSE should also provide order handling comparisons with common order types to show how traditional limit orders and hidden orders are disadvantaged by the features discussed above. NYSE's submission is of concern to the problem of equity market structure as it will create precedent on the issues disclosed, many of which could harm the marketplace as a whole by continuing to provide features that are tuned to the needs of high-volume / low-latency traders.

Postscript

Acting through its Division of Trading and Markets, the SEC ultimately approved the proposed rule changes for both NYSE and NYSE MKT, finding them consistent with the requirements of the Securities Exchange Act of 1934 and the requirements for ISOs established by Regulation NMS.[23] Among other things, the Division of Trading and Markets maintained that "[t]he ALO modifier for day limit orders is designed to be used to provide liquidity on the Exchanges at aggressive prices, rather than to remove liquidity" and "the requirement that an ALO limit order have a minimum size of one round lot should reduce the economic incentives for a submitting firm to attempt to use this order type to detect the presence of hidden interest."[24] Moreover, the Division of Trading and Markets dismissed the view that "the ALO modifier for limit orders would provide unjustified queue priority or that it would encourage the submission of orders that are not bona fide."[25] While

---

[23] Order Approving Proposed Rule Changes by New York Stock Exchange LLC and NYSE MKT LLC Amending Exchange Rule 13 to Make the Add Liquidity Only Modifier Available for Limit Orders, and Make the Day Time-in-Force Condition and Add Liquidity Only Modifier Available for Intermarket Sweep Orders, Exchange Act Release No. 73,333, 79 Fed. Reg. 62,223 (Oct. 9, 2014), *available at* http://www.gpo.gov/fdsys/pkg/FR-2014-10-16/pdf/2014-24547.pdf.
[24] *Id.* at 62,226.
[25] *Id.*

this approval is consistent with the SEC's deference to the industry's rulemaking initiatives, it should also be noted that the regulators addressed improper use of the post-only ISO order type in contravention of Regulation NMS in its later enforcement action against Latour Trading.[26]

---

[26] Latour Trading LLC, Exchange Act Release No. 76,029 (Sept. 30, 2015), http://www.sec.gov/litigation/admin/2015/34-76029.pdf.

X. The Flash Boys Lawsuit: The End of the Beginning?

Haim Bodek and Stanislav Dolgopolov
Decimus Capital Markets, LLC
October 2015

The dismissal of the *City of Providence v. BATS* class action lawsuit[1] serves as a landmark in the market structure conundrum. After all, this lawsuit targeted almost every securities exchange in the equities space, contained grave allegations of securities fraud, and demanded radical structural changes for the architecture of securities markets. While the lawsuit's dismissal is currently being appealed and similar allegations may still be reanimated or repackaged in some form, the federal district court's decision is seen as a big win for securities exchanges and HFTs. If this decision stands on appeal, it would look like a decisive victory for these constituencies on the legal issues of the immunity shield afforded to securities exchanges and the lack of demonstrated harm to investors stemming from a range of widespread practices. At the same time, the securities industry may just find itself fighting in Round Two.

The initial version of this lawsuit was filed just weeks after the release of *Flash Boys* by Michael Lewis in March of 2014.[2] Although a lawsuit with very similar allegations could have been brought on the basis of a variety of public sources well before the book's release, the publicity surrounding *Flash Boys* certainly served as a catalyst. Not surprisingly, the term "Flash Boys Lawsuit" entered into the narrative of the market structure debate, and the initial complaint did in fact rely heavily on the book, quoting various passages and utilizing the taxonomy of alleged abuses, such as

---

[1] *In re* Barclays Liquidity Cross & High Frequency Trading Litig., No. 14-MD-2589 (JMF), 2015 U.S. Dist. LEXIS 113323 (S.D.N.Y. Aug. 26, 2015).
[2] *See* MICHAEL LEWIS, FLASH BOYS: A WALL STREET REVOLT (2014).

"electronic front-running," "rebate arbitrage," and "slow-market arbitrage."[3] The complaint was subsequently amended, limiting the broad scope of its initial allegations and zeroing in on the leading equities exchanges and Barclays' dark pool.[4] Furthermore, the amended complaint expanded its coverage of the so-called "order type controversy," frequently citing the arguments developed by Mr. Bodek in his critique of HFT order types.

Judge Jesse M. Furman dismissed the Flash Boys Lawsuit in its entirety on August 26, 2015, while bundling it with an additional lawsuit against Barclays based on state law claims. Overall, the court held that the securities exchanges were protected from private lawsuits by the *doctrine of regulatory immunity* afforded to these trading venues under the Securities Exchange Act of 1934, which the court applied to private data feeds and complex order types. Even more importantly, the court essentially ruled on the merits from the standpoint of investor harm, concluding that that no valid claim had been articulated. At the same time, the ruling left room for the continuing public debate about the phenomenon of HFT as a market reform issue: "[T]he Court's task in deciding the present motions was not to wade into the larger public debate about HFT that was sparked by Michael Lewis's book *Flash Boys*. Lewis and the critics of HFT may be right in arguing that it serves no productive purpose and merely allows certain traders to exploit technological inefficiencies in the markets at the expense of other traders."[5]

One of the pivotal legal issues in the Flash Boys Lawsuit addressed the boundaries of regulatory immunity that shelters securities exchanges as self-regulatory organizations from private lawsuits for

---

[3] Complaint for Violation of the Federal Securities Laws, City of Providence, R.I. v. BATS Global Mkts., Inc., No. 1:14-cv-2811 para 6, at 3 (S.D.N.Y. Apr. 18, 2014).
[4] *See* Second Consolidated Amended Complaint for Violation of the Federal Securities Laws, City of Providence, R.I. v. BATS Global Mkts., Inc., No. 1:14-cv-02811-JMF (Nov. 24, 2014).
[5] *In re Barclays Liquidity Cross & High Frequency Trading*, 2015 U.S. Dist. LEXIS 113323, at *82.

their official actions. This issue is critical when considered in light of symbiotic relationships between securities exchanges and preferred market participants, which, as extensively discussed by Mr. Bodek, have resulted in various forms of preferential treatment for HFTs' trading strategies.[6] Relying on the traditionally broad interpretation of the scope of self-regulation, the court reaffirmed the doctrine of regulatory immunity, with the "exclusively non-regulatory" test being adopted to separate protected regulatory from non-protected commercial activities.[7]

Definitively, the court held that "the Exchanges are absolutely immune from suit based on their creation of complex order types and provision of proprietary data feeds, both of which fall within the scope of the quasi-governmental powers delegated to the Exchanges."[8] By contrast, the court arrived at the provocative conclusion that "it is hard to see how the provision of co-location services serves a regulatory function or differs from the provision of commercial products and services that courts have held not to be protected by absolute immunity in other cases. . . . The Exchanges, therefore, are not immune from suit based on the provision of co-location services."[9] On some level, the court's distinction between co-location services and complex order types / private data feeds appears artificial. For one thing, such offerings as private data feeds, complex order types, and co-location services are typically used in combination to unlock specific exchange-provided features—most commonly, to secure a top-of-queue position on an exchange's order book ahead of other market participants. Moreover, the SEC has already established a track record in ensuring that co-location

---

[6] HAIM BODEK, THE PROBLEM OF HFT: COLLECTED WRITINGS ON HIGH FREQUENCY TRADING & STOCK MARKET STRUCTURE REFORM (2013), *available at* http://www.amazon.com/gp/product/B00B1UDSS4.
[7] *In re Barclays Liquidity Cross & High Frequency Trading*, 2015 U.S. Dist. LEXIS 113323, at *30, 36, 38.
[8] *Id.* at *38–39.
[9] *Id.* at *31.

services are provided pursuant to the proper rulemaking procedures, including the regulatory agency's own review and approval.[10]

Turning to other definitional nuances, one may look at the court's extension of immunity to the defendant exchanges in connection with complex order types: "[T]he order types permitted by an Exchange define the ways in which traders can interact with that Exchange. By establishing a defined set of order types, the Exchanges police the ways in which users of an exchange are able to interact with each other."[11] Once again, a comparison with co-location services is appropriate: the question is whether such services also involve "interaction" of market participants with the exchange in question and among each other. In any instance, the court established that a borderline between "regulation" and "products" may not exist at all. Take, for instance, the court's position on the regulatory nature of some products with a reference to order types: "Where—as is the case with the complex order types at issue here—the act of creating a product has a regulatory dimension, an exchange is immune from suit based on that product."[12] Looking forward, this distinction between regulatory and non-regulatory products offered by securities exchanges provides an arena for further legal arguments aimed at the evolving suite of functionalities in the modern electronic marketplace. One can anticipate skillful, if not hair-thin, characterizations by plaintiffs alleging harm from such products and defendants offering them. For instance, one may ponder on the nature of routing services provided by securities exchanges, potentially involving the best execution dimension, although SEC-approved liability disclaimers may come into play.[13]

---

[10] *See, e.g.*, N.Y. Stock Exch. LLC, Exchange Act Release No. 72,065 (May 1, 2014), http://www.sec.gov/litigation/admin/2014/34-72065.pdf.

[11] *In re Barclays Liquidity Cross & High Frequency Trading*, 2015 U.S. Dist. LEXIS 113323, at *31–32 (internal citation omitted).

[12] *Id.* at *33.

[13] As an illustration, the limitations on liability of NASDAQ Market Center, which, in its turn, routes orders to other destinations through Nasdaq Execution Services, are described in Rule 4626. *See NASDAQ Stock Market Rules*,

Although the doctrine of regulatory immunity sheltering securities exchanges had been a high hurdle from the very beginning, the dismissal of the claims against Barclays in connection with its dark pool was not so widely anticipated. As categorically stated by the court, "[T]he . . . claims against Barclays fail because they do not allege reasonable reliance."[14] However, another private lawsuit brought on behalf of Barclays' *shareholders*, as opposed to public investors more generally in the Flash Boys Lawsuit, did survive the motion to dismiss with respect to "the alleged nature of the fraud [that] Barclays was touting the safety of LX while at the same time courting predatory firms."[15] Additionally, as suggested by the settlement with UBS,[16] dark pools may be exposed for their order type-related practices, and charges of securities fraud in private lawsuits are certainly possible. The controversy surrounding ITG's secret proprietary trading desk adds to the list of wrongful practices that have been discovered inside dark pools.[17] In fact, ITG is already being sued by its shareholders, and the sheer drop in its stock price in the aftermath of these revelations suggests the seriousness and tangibility of the applicable harm.[18]

Another important theme raised in the Flash Boys Lawsuit pertains to the nature of market manipulation, which is properly defined as an interference with price discovery and a generator of artificial price movements. Indeed, the court rejected the manipulative-scheme claim as the chief theory of liability, pointing to this relatively narrow legal definition of market manipulation. More

---

NASDAQ OMX GRP., INC., http://nasdaq.cchwallstreet.com (follow "Rule 4000" hyperlink) (last visited Sept. 26, 2015).

[14] *In re Barclays Liquidity Cross & High Frequency Trading*, 2015 U.S. Dist. LEXIS 113323, at *52.

[15] Strougo v. Barclays PLC, No. 14-cv-5797 (SAS), 2015 U.S. Dist. LEXIS 54059, at *44 (S.D.N.Y. Apr. 24, 2015).

[16] UBS Sec. LLC, Securities Act Release No. 9697, Exchange Act Release No. 74,060 (Jan. 15, 2015), http://www.sec.gov/litigation/admin/2015/33-9697.pdf.

[17] For the settlement between the SEC and ITG, see ITG Inc., Securities Act Release No. 9887, Exchange Act Release No. 75,672 (Aug. 12, 2015), http://www.sec.gov/litigation/admin/2015/33-9887.pdf.

[18] *See, e.g.*, Class Action Complaint, Bernacchi v. Inv. Tech Grp., Inc., No. 1:15-cv-06369-JFK (S.D.N.Y. Aug. 12, 2015).

generally, the scope of securities fraud is much wider than market manipulation. Consider that *riding price changes* with the assistance of inadequately documented functionalities is different from *creating artificial price patterns* in order to profit from them, which is the essence of market manipulation. Note, however, that even the first scenario may be classified as an instance of securities fraud to the extent that false or misleading statements have been made by trading venues or perhaps, in some instances, by HFTs themselves in order to exploit non-transparent or inaccurately described functionalities. It should be stressed that the amended complaint did push the point of deficient disclosure by the securities exchanges with respect to complex order types and provided a taxonomy of investor harm from such order type-related practices.[19]

Putting aside securities exchanges protected by the shield of regulatory immunity and liability disclaimers in their rules, private lawsuits are likely to play an important role in challenging industry practices that disadvantage investors, while complementing the regulators' limited enforcement resources. The "rigged markets" paradigm is not particularly helpful, but recent enforcement actions suggest that there is a range of rogue players, corrupt practices, and disclosure deficiencies that have yet to be thoroughly addressed. One obvious area of potential liability is represented by maker-taker and payment for order flow practices of retail brokerage firms, and one current case, *Klein v. TD Ameritrade*, is significant in terms of the court's future assessment of the viability and accuracy of the plaintiffs' allegations. These allegations rely on a consistent theory of harm from the standpoint of the duty of best execution, which leverages one of the better-known empirical studies, while making additional claims about orders marked as "retail" when routed to securities exchanges that use "retail attribution programs."[20] Moreover, wholesalers, i.e.,

---

[19] *See* Second Consolidated Amended Complaint for Violation of the Federal Securities Laws, City of Providence, R.I. v. BATS Global Mkts., Inc., No. 1:14-cv-02811-JMF paras. 137–40, at 67–69 (Nov. 24, 2014).

[20] *See* Amended Class Action Complaint for Violations of Federal Securities Laws, Klein v. TD Ameritrade Holding Corp., No. 8:14-cv-00396-JFB-TDT (Apr. 14, 2015). The empirical study in question is Robert Battalio et al., Can Brokers Have It All? On the Relation Between Make-Take Fees and Limit Order Execution Quality (Mar. 31, 2015) (unpublished manuscript), *available at* http://ssrn.com/abstract=2367462.

off-exchange market makers, may be exposed based on their agency functions that may translate to the duty of best execution, such as the one owed by front-end brokers. Likewise, rogue players in the HFT space might be held liable for a range of activities amounting to securities fraud, whether for activities classified as market manipulation or for deliberate violations of the multitude of trading rules.

While the Flash Boys Lawsuit's dismissal surely looks like a setback for private litigants in the market structure space, it is only the end of the beginning. Some private lawsuits in this space *will* result in ever increasing awards or settlements, reputational damage, and career-ending outcomes for some executives. Moreover, even unsuccessful lawsuits may end up being a vehicle of market reform in terms of regulatory scrutiny and commercial pressure. Overall, for a lawsuit to be successful, it is critical to frame the underlying harm, fit it within the existing doctrinal boundaries of securities law, and quantify its magnitude with a practical model for assessing damages. Accordingly, it would be prudent to reinforce even early-stage filings—just to keep such claims alive—with proprietary models that replicate the processes through which defendants monetize wrongful practices.

In our assessment, successful lawsuits are likely to focus on deficient disclosure rather than the essence of "unfair" practices, with the latter being more appropriate for market reform rather than liability. Despite the complexity of disclosure relating to the modern electronic marketplace and the persistent problem of having to demonstrate investor reliance, it is hard to deny the materiality, that is, profitability, of a range of practices attributed to deficient disclosure. The corresponding harm to investors is quite tangible when one examines the details of asymmetries currently operational in the modern electronic marketplace. Shining some sunlight on practices that harm investors, as exemplified by the wave of order type-related disclosures and filings mandated by the regulators in 2014, is still a reliable disinfectant, as well as a restraint on profits. Moreover, lawsuits brought by a target's *shareholders* rather than *market participants* in general may be in a more advantageous position of demonstrating harm. For the former, such harm could be proxied by market reaction to corrective disclosures, while the latter are burdened with the more difficult task of demonstrating the mechanics of the abuse in question and quantifying their own economic exposure.

Finally, one has to be mindful of the continuing pileup of enforcement actions in the market structure space, as well as pros and cons of "front-running" the regulators. Not uncommonly, successful private lawsuits piggyback on enforcement actions, and the regulators' activity in this space is an enormous litigation risk by itself.[21] On the other hand, that factor failed to work either way in the Flash Boys Lawsuit. More specifically, the court dismissed the claims against Barclays largely based on the lawsuit brought by the New York Attorney General.[22] Likewise, the SEC's enforcement action against Direct Edge,[23] though it came too late to be referenced in the final version of the complaint, would not have provided sufficient firepower to pass the high hurdle of regulatory immunity in connection with order type-related practices.

---

[21] As an illustration, the recent market structure-related settlement between the SEC and Latour Trading, which addressed, among other things, improper use of post-only intermarket sweep orders, contained the provision that the respondent would not be allowed to offset the civil penalty in any related private lawsuit. *See* Latour Trading LLC, Exchange Act Release No. 76,029, at 16-17 (Sept. 30, 2015), http://www.sec.gov/litigation/admin/2015/34-76029.pdf.

[22] Complaint, New York v. Barclays Capital, Inc., No. 451391/2014 (N.Y. Sup. Ct. June 25, 2014).

[23] EDGA Exch. Inc., Exchange Act Release No. 74,032, at 3 (Jan. 12, 2015), http://www.sec.gov/litigation/admin/2015/34-74032.pdf.

Appendix A: Summary of Key Enforcement Actions and Lawsuits

SEC settlement with the New York Stock Exchange and NYSE Euronext (Sept. 14, 2012)

Risks highlighted: systems controls, information integrity

Source: N.Y. Stock Exch. LLC, Exchange Act Release No. 67,857 (Sept. 14, 2012), http://www.sec.gov/litigation/admin/2012/34-67857.pdf

---

SEC settlement with eBX, LLC (Oct. 3, 2012)

Risks highlighted: systems controls, confidentiality of customer information

Source: eBX, LLC, Exchange Act Release No. 67,969 (Oct. 3, 2012), http://www.sec.gov/litigation/admin/2012/34-67969.pdf

---

SEC settlement with Biremis Corporation and its owners / founders (Dec. 18, 2012)

Risks highlighted: systems controls, market access, market manipulation

Source: Biremis Corp., Exchange Act Release No. 68,456 (Dec. 18, 2012), http://www.sec.gov/litigation/admin/2012/34-68456.pdf

SEC settlement with NASDAQ Stock Market and NASDAQ Execution Services (May 29, 2013)

Risks highlighted: systems controls, order handling

Source: NASDAQ Stock Mkt., LLC, Exchange Act Release No. 69,655 (May 29, 2013), http://www.sec.gov/litigation/admin/2013/34-69655.pdf

SEC settlement with the Chicago Board Options Exchange and C2 Options Exchange (June 11, 2013)

Risks highlighted: failure to enforce rules, internal controls, order handling

Source: Chi. Bd. Options Exch., Inc., Exchange Act Release No. 69,726 (June 11, 2013), http://www.sec.gov/litigation/admin/2013/34-69726.pdf

SEC settlement with the Chicago Stock Exchange (Aug. 15, 2013)

Risks highlighted: systems controls

Source: Chi. Stock Exch., Inc., Exchange Act Release No. 70,214 (Aug. 15, 2013), http://www.sec.gov/litigation/admin/2013/34-70214.pdf

SEC settlement with Knight Capital (Oct. 16, 2013)

Risks highlighted: systems controls, market access

Source: Knight Capital Ams. LLC, Exchange Act Release No. 70,694 (Oct. 16, 2013), http://www.sec.gov/litigation/admin/2013/34-70694.pdf

SEC settlement with ConvergEx Group's affiliates (Dec. 18, 2013)

Risks highlighted: systems controls, market access, undisclosed markups

Source: G-Trade Servs. LLC, Exchange Act Release No. 71,128, Investment Advisers Act Release No. 3744 (Dec. 18, 2013), http://www.sec.gov/litigation/admin/2013/34-71128.pdf

---

Class action lawsuit against CME Group, CBOT, and several executives (Apr. 11, 2014)

Risks highlighted: selective disclosure, market manipulation

Source: Second Amended Class Action Complaint, Braman v. CME Grp., Inc., No. 1:14-cv-02646 (N.D. Ill. July 22, 2014)

Class action lawsuit against the equities exchanges and Barclays (Apr. 18, 2014)

Risks highlighted: selective disclosure, false and misleading disclosure, order handling

Sources: Complaint for Violation of the Federal Securities Laws, City of Providence, R.I. v. BATS Global Mkts., Inc., No. 1:14-cv-2811 (S.D.N.Y. Apr. 18, 2014); Second Consolidated Amended Complaint for Violation of the Federal Securities Laws, City of Providence, R.I. v. BATS Global Mkts., Inc., No. 1:14-cv-02811-JMF (Nov. 24, 2014); In re Barclays Liquidity Cross & High Frequency Trading Litig., No. 14-MD-2589 (JMF), 2015 U.S. Dist. LEXIS 113323 (S.D.N.Y. Aug. 26, 2015)

Settlements / Agreements between the New York Attorney General and several news distribution firms (July 2013 – Apr. 2014)

Risks highlighted: preferential treatment

Sources: Press Release, N.Y. State Attorney Gen., A.G. Schneiderman Secures Agreement by Thomson Reuters to Stop Offering Early Access to Market-Moving Information (July 8, 2013), http://www.ag.ny.gov/press-release/ag-schneiderman-secures-agreement-thomson-reuters-stop-offering-early-access-market; Press Release, N.Y. State Attorney Gen., A.G. Schneiderman Announces Marketwired Agreement to End Sales of News Feeds to High-Frequency Traders (Mar. 19, 2014), http://www.ag.ny.gov/press-release/ag-schneiderman-announces-marketwired-agreement-end-sales-news-feeds-high-frequency; Press Release, N.Y. State Attorney Gen., A.G. Schneiderman Announces Unprecedented Steps by News Distribution Firm to Curb Preferential Access for High-Frequency Traders (Apr. 30, 2014), http://www.ag.ny.gov/press-release/ag-schneiderman-announces-unprecedented-steps-news-distribution-firm-curb-preferential

---

SEC settlement with the New York Stock Exchange, NYSE Arca, and NYSE MKT (May 1, 2014)

Risks highlighted: systems controls, false and misleading disclosure, order handling

Source: N.Y. Stock Exch. LLC, Exchange Act Release No. 72,065 (May 1, 2014), http://www.sec.gov/litigation/admin/2014/34-72065.pdf

---

Class action lawsuit against securities exchanges in connection with market data (May 23, 2014)

Risks highlighted: information integrity, breach of contract

Sources: Amended Class Action Complaint, Lanier v. BATS Exch., Inc., No. 1:14-cv-03745 (S.D.N.Y. Aug. 15, 2014); Lanier v. BATS

Exch., Inc., Nos. 14-cv-3745 (KBF),14-cv-3865 (KBF),14-cv-3866 (KBF), 2015 U.S. Dist. LEXIS 55954 (S.D.N.Y. Apr. 28, 2015)

SEC settlement with Liquidnet (June 6, 2014)

Risks highlighted: false and misleading disclosure, confidentiality of customer information

Source: Liquidnet, Inc., Securities Act Release No. 9596, Exchange Act Release No. 72,339 (June 6, 2014), http://www.sec.gov/litigation/admin/2014/33-9596.pdf

New York Attorney General's complaint against Barclays Capital in connection with its dark pool (June 25, 2014)

Risks highlighted: selective disclosure, false and misleading disclosure

Source: Complaint, New York v. Barclays Capital, Inc., No. 451391/2014 (N.Y. Sup. Ct. June 25, 2014)

SEC settlement with LavaFlow (July 25, 2014)

Risks highlighted: confidentiality of customer information

Source: LavaFlow, Inc., Exchange Act Release No. 72,673 (July 25, 2014), http://www.sec.gov/litigation/admin/2014/34-72673.pdf

Class action lawsuit against TD Ameritrade Holding Corporation, TD Ameritrade, Inc, and their executive (Sept. 15, 2014)

Risks highlighted: conflicts of interest, best execution

Source: Amended Class Action Complaint for Violations of Federal Securities Laws, Klein v. TD Ameritrade Holding Corp., No. 8:14-cv-00396-JFB-TDT (Apr. 14, 2015)

SEC settlement with Latour Trading and its executive (Sept. 17, 2014)

Risks highlighted: systems controls

Source: Latour Trading LLC, Exchange Act Release No. 73,125 (Sept. 17, 2014), http://www.sec.gov/litigation/admin/2014/34-73125.pdf

---

SEC settlement with Athena Capital Research, LLC (Oct. 16, 2014)

Risks Highlighted: market manipulation

Source: Athena Capital Research, LLC, Exchange Act Release No. 73,369, Investment Advisers Release No. 3950 (Oct. 16, 2014), http://www.sec.gov/litigation/admin/2014/34-73369.pdf

---

SEC settlement with Wedbush Securities and its executives (Nov. 20, 2014)

Risks highlighted: systems controls, market access, market manipulation

Source: Wedbush Sec. Inc., Exchange Act Release No. 73,652, Investment Advisers Act Release No. 3971 (Nov. 20, 2014), http://www.sec.gov/litigation/admin/2014/34-73654.pdf

---

SEC settlement with Morgan Stanley (Dec. 10, 2014)

Risks highlighted: systems controls, market access

Source: Morgan Stanley & Co., Exchange Act Release No. 73,802 (Dec. 10, 2014), http://www.sec.gov/litigation/admin/2014/34-73802.pdf

SEC settlement with Direct Edge's exchanges (Jan. 12, 2015)

Risks highlighted: selective disclosure, false and misleading disclosure, order handling

Source: EDGA Exch. Inc., Exchange Act Release No. 74,032 (Jan. 12, 2015), http://www.sec.gov/litigation/admin/2015/34-74032.pdf

SEC complaint against an organizer of a spoofing / layering scheme

Risks highlighted: market manipulation, market access

Source: Complaint, SEC v. Milrud, No. 2:15-cv-00237-KM-SCM (D.N.J. Jan. 13, 2015)

SEC settlement with UBS Securities (Jan. 15, 2015)

Risks highlighted: selective disclosure, false and misleading disclosure, subpenny pricing

Source: UBS Sec. LLC, Securities Act Release No. 9697, Exchange Act Release No. 74,060 (Jan. 15, 2015), http://www.sec.gov/litigation/admin/2015/33-9697.pdf

SEC settlement with ITG Inc. and its affiliate (Aug. 12, 2015)

Risks highlighted: false and misleading disclosure, confidentiality of customer information

Source: ITG Inc., Securities Act Release No. 9887, Exchange Act Release No. 75,672 (Aug. 12, 2015), http://www.sec.gov/litigation/admin/2015/33-9887.pdf

---

SEC settlement with Citigroup Global Markets (Aug. 19, 2015)

Risks highlighted: systems controls

Source: Citigroup Global Mkts., Inc., Exchange Act Release No. 75729, Investment Advisors Act Release No. 4178 (Aug. 19, 2015), http://www.sec.gov/litigation/admin/2015/34-75729.pdf

---

SEC settlement with Latour Trading (Sept. 30, 2015)

Risks highlighted: order handling, systems controls

Source: Latour Trading LLC, Exchange Act Release No. 76,029 (Sept. 30, 2015), http://www.sec.gov/litigation/admin/2015/34-76029.pdf

Appendix B: Selected Market Structure-Related References

Congressional Hearings

The Role of Regulation in Shaping Equity Market Structure and Electronic Trading: Hearing Before the S. Comm. on Banking, Hous., & Urban Affairs, 113th Cong. (2015), *available at* http://www.gpo.gov/fdsys/pkg/CHRG-113shrg91300/pdf/CHRG-113shrg91300.pdf

Conflicts of Interest, Investor Loss of Confidence, and High Speed Trading in U.S. Stock Markets, Hearing Before the Permanent Subcomm. on Investigations of the S. Comm. on Homeland Sec. & Governmental Affairs, 113th Cong. (2014), *available at* http://www.gpo.gov/fdsys/pkg/CHRG-113shrg89752/pdf/CHRG-113shrg89752.pdf

Computerized Trading: What Should the Rules of the Road Be? – Part II: Hearing Before the Subcomm. on Sec., Ins., & Inv. of the S. Comm. on Banking, Hous., & Urban Affairs, 112th Cong. (2013), *available at* http://www.gpo.gov/fdsys/pkg/CHRG-112shrg80273/pdf/CHRG-112shrg80273.pdf

Computerized Trading: What Should the Rules of the Road Be? – Part I: Hearing Before the Subcomm. on Sec., Ins., & Inv. of the S. Comm. on Banking, Hous., & Urban Affairs, 112th Cong. 47 (2013), *available at* http://www.gpo.gov/fdsys/pkg/CHRG-112shrg80168/pdf/CHRG-112shrg80168.pdf

Market Structure: Ensuring Orderly, Efficient, Innovative and Competitive Markets for Issuers and Investors: Hearing Before the Subcomm. on Capital Mkts. & Gov't Sponsored Enters. of the H.

Comm. on Fin. Servs., 112th Cong. (2013), *available at* http://www.gpo.gov/fdsys/pkg/CHRG-112hhrg76108/pdf/CHRG-112hhrg76108.pdf

Key Policy-Oriented Speeches, Other Statements, and Analysis by the SEC

Luis A. Aguilar, Comm'r, U.S. Sec. & Exch. Comm'n, U.S. Equity Market Structure: Making Our Markets Work Better for Investors (May 11, 2015), http://www.sec.gov/news/statement/us-equity-market-structure.html

Memorandum from the SEC Div. of Trading & Mkts. to the SEC Mkt. Structure Advisory Comm. (April 30, 2015), https://www.sec.gov/spotlight/emsac/memo-rule-611-regulation-nms.pdf

Letter from Mary Jo White, Chairman, U.S. Sec. & Exch. Comm'n, to Sen. Tim Johnson, Chairman & Sen. Mike Crapo, Ranking Minority Member, Comm. on Hous., Banking & Urb. Affairs, U.S. Senate (Dec. 23, 2014), http://www.securitytraders.org/wp-content/uploads/2014/12/JOHNSON-CRAPO-EQUITY-MARKET-STRUCTURE-ES152784-Response.pdf

Mary Jo White, Chairman, U.S. Sec. & Exch. Comm'n, Enhancing Our Equity Market Structure: Remarks at Sandler O'Neill & Partners, L.P. Global Exchange and Brokerage Conference (June 5, 2014), http://www.sec.gov/News/Speech/Detail/Speech/1370542004312#.U99FBGN5WEc

White Papers, Policy Papers, and Industry Commentary

PHIL MACKINTOSH, KCG HOLDINGS, INC., DEMYSTIFYING ORDER TYPES (Sept. 2014), *available at* http://www.kcg.com//uploads/documents/KCG_Demystifying-Order-Types_092414.pdf

MICAH HAUPTMAN, CONSUMER FED. OF AM., TOWARD A U.S. EQUITY MARKET STRUCTURE THAT SERVES ALL INVESTORS (2014), http://www.consumerfed.org/pdfs/CFA-Market-Structure-White-Paper.pdf

SIFMA BD. COMM. ON EQUITY MKT. STRUCTURE, RECOMMENDATIONS AS OF JULY 10, 2014 (2014), *available at* http://www.sifma.org/issues/item.aspx?id=8589949840

BLACKROCK, US EQUITY MARKET STRUCTURE: AN INVESTOR'S PERSPECTIVE (April 2014), https://www.blackrock.com/corporate/en-us/literature/whitepaper/viewpoint-us-equity-market-structure-april-2014.pdf

TRADEWORX, INC., PUBLIC COMMENTARY ON SEC MARKET STRUCTURE CONCEPT RELEASE (Apr. 21, 2010), https://www.sec.gov/comments/s7-02-10/s70210-129.pdf

Selected Publications by the Authors

Stanislav Dolgopolov, *Regulating Merchants of Liquidity: Market Making from Crowded Floors to High-Frequency Trading*, U. PA. J. BUS. L. (forthcoming), *available at* http://ssrn.com/abstract=2677087

Haim Bodek & Stanislav Dolgopolov, *BATS' Exclusive Listing Proposal a Reasonable and Cautious Step*, TABB FORUM (Apr. 17, 2015), http://tabbforum.com/opinions/bats%27-exclusive-listing-proposal-a-reasonable-and-cautious-step (registration required)

Stanislav Dolgopolov, *The Maker-Taker Pricing Model and Its Impact on the Securities Market Structure: A Can of Worms for Securities Fraud?*, 8 VA. L. & BUS. REV. 231 (2014), *available at* http://ssrn.com/abstract=2399821

Haim Bodek & Stanislav Dolgopolov, *Resolving the Order Type Controversy: A Logical Conclusion?*, TABB FORUM (May 21, 2014), http://tabbforum.com/opinions/resolving-the-order-type-controversy (registration required)

Stanislav Dolgopolov, *High-Frequency Trading, Order Types, and the Evolution of the Securities Market Structure: One Whistleblower's Consequences for Securities Regulation*, 2014 U. ILL. J.L. TECH. & POL'Y 145, *available at* http://ssrn.com/abstract=2314574

Haim Bodek, *The Order Type Controversy, Part I: Price to Comply*, TABB FORUM (Mar. 10, 2014), http://tabbforum.com/opinions/the-order-type-controversy-part-i-price-to-comply (registration required)

Stanislav Dolgopolov, *Linking the Securities Market Structure and Capital Formation: Incentives for Market Makers?*, 16 U. PA. J. BUS. L. 1 (2013), *available at* http://ssrn.com/abstract=2169601

Stanislav Dolgopolov, *Providing Liquidity in a High-Frequency World: Trading Obligations and Privileges of Market Makers and a Private Right of Action*, 7 BROOK. J. CORP. FIN. & COM. L. 303 (2013), *available at* http://ssrn.com/abstract=2032134

HAIM BODEK, THE PROBLEM OF HFT: COLLECTED WRITINGS ON HIGH FREQUENCY TRADING & STOCK MARKET STRUCTURE REFORM (2013), *available at* http://www.amazon.com/gp/product/B00B1UDSS4

Stanislav Dolgopolov, *Insider Trading, Informed Trading, and Market Making: Liquidity of Securities Markets in the Zero-Sum Game*, 3 WM. & MARY BUS. L. REV. 1 (2012), *available at* http://ssrn.com/abstract=1779189

Stanislav Dolgopolov, *A Two-Sided Loyalty?: Exploring the Boundaries of Fiduciary Duties of Market Makers*, 12 U.C. DAVIS BUS. L.J. 31 (2011), *available at* http://ssrn.com/abstract=1920242

Available: A Comprehensive Proprietary Research Report on the Market Structure Crisis

The Market Structure Crisis in the U.S. Securities Industry in 2015 and Beyond: Navigating Regulatory Uncertainty in Rapidly Evolving Markets and the Continuing Pressure on High-Frequency Trading

> DECIMUS CAPITAL MARKETS, LLC
>
> DCM
>
> **The Market Structure Crisis in the U.S. Securities Industry in 2015 and Beyond**
> Navigating Regulatory Uncertainty in Rapidly Evolving Markets and the Continuing Pressure on High-Frequency Trading
> Research Report Outline
> Full Report Available Now - Updated to Reflect Current Developments
> **Haim Bodek and Stanislav Dolgopolov**

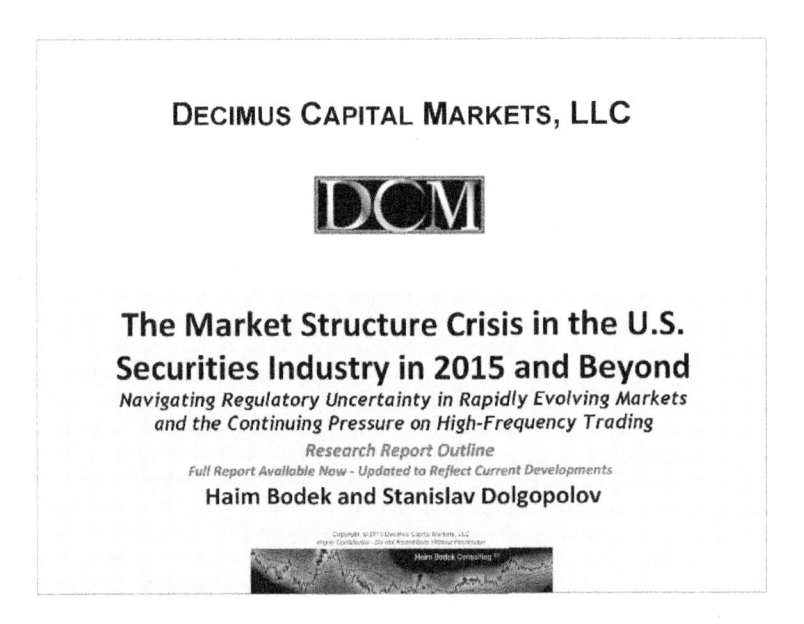

- Offers a comprehensive resource for regulatory, legal, and competitive developments related to the market structure crisis
- Enhances the chapters of this book with concise summaries
- Provides additional chapters covering

- - The significance of the market structure crisis
  - The evolving landscape and state of the HFT industry
  - Regulation of market data distribution
  - Regulation of market makers
- Provides detailed summaries for key enforcement actions, investigations, court cases, and lawsuits in 2011-2015
- Continuously updated to reflect current developments
- Includes a customized presentation and additional consulting hours by Haim Bodek and Stanislav Dolgopolov

Contact information:

Haim Bodek – Managing Principal
Decimus Capital Markets, LLC
203-359-2625
haim@haimbodek.com
http://haimbodek.com
https://decimuscapitalmarkets.com

Available: Haim Bodek's *The Problem of HFT*

Paperback: The Problem of HFT (paperback)
E-book: The Problem of HFT (e-book)

"Today the US Equities market is comprised of 13 Exchanges, 50 dark pools and a host of internalizing brokers. ... Haim Bodek has both been on the front lines of understanding the penalties of not fully comprehending this complexity, but also helping bring this complexity to light. This book is a must read by anyone attempting to fully understand the challenges of professionally competing in today's complex and challenging electronic trading environment."
- **Larry Tabb , Founder & CEO Tabb Group**

"This is a must-read for any trader in the markets. It's that simple. Mr. Bodek is shining a light onto the troubling games and unfair practices that have actually come to serve as the foundation of our high speed marketplace."
- Sal Arnuk, Co-Founder Themis Trading LLC & Co-Author Broken Markets

"Haim Bodek lays out the problems created by the explosion of High Frequency Trading."
- Ted Kaufman, Fmr. U.S. Senator from Delaware

This book explores the problem of high frequency trading (HFT) as well as the need for US stock market reform. This collection of previously published and unpublished materials includes the following articles and white papers:

1. **The Problem of HFT** - explains how HFTs came to dominate US equity markets by exploiting artificial advantages introduced by electronic exchanges that catered to HFT strategies
2. **HFT Scalping Strategies** - describes the primary features of modern HFT strategies currently active in US equities as well as the benefits these strategies extract from the maker-taker market model and the regulatory framework of the national market system
3. **Why HFTs Have an Advantage** - explains the critical importance of HFT-oriented special order types and exchange order matching engine practices in the operation of modern HFT strategies
4. **HFT - A Systemic Issue** - a discussion of the latest industry and regulatory developments with regard to exchange order matching practices that serve to advantage HFTs over the public customer
5. **Electronic Liquidity Strategy** - proposes a conceptual framework for institutional traders to achieve superior execution performance in HFT-oriented electronic market venues
6. **Reforming the National Market System** - proposes a 10-step plan for strengthening the operation of the US equities

marketplace in order to serve the needs of long-term investors
7. **NZZ Interview with Haim Bodek** - addresses current topics and proposals for US equities market structure reforms
8. **TradeTech Interview with Haim Bodek** - addresses the current status of the HFT special order type debate

"Modern HFT wasn't a paradigm shift because its innovations brought new efficiencies into the marketplace. HFT was a paradigm shift because its innovations proved that anti-competitive barriers to entry could be erected in the market structure itself to preference one class of market participant above all others."

About Decimus Capital Markets, LLC and Its Offerings

Decimus Capital Markets, LLC ("DCM"), which was founded by HFT whistleblower and electronic trader Haim Bodek, specializes in the inner workings of the modern electronic marketplace. DCM's offerings include the following:

Electronic Trading Strategy

We assist proprietary trading firms, hedge funds, and investment banks in navigating the inherent complexity of the modern electronic marketplace, providing expert services and solutions tailored for electronic equities, options and futures markets. Our core competencies include algorithmic execution, quantitative strategy, systematic trading, systems architecture, risk management, and compliance.

We serve some of the most sophisticated trading firms in the world with our research products and execution strategy consulting services, providing a critical role in assisting our clients in adapting their strategies to market structure change. Client confidentiality is of utmost importance to us. We manage our relationships with discretion and manage our staff on a need-to-know basis.

Markets and Regulation

We assist institutional investors, broker-dealers, and proprietary trading firms in navigating the complexity of the security industry's market structure and relevant regulatory risks. Our clients leverage our expertise through customized research reports and consulting services addressing market structure and its regulation, with an emphasis on competitive, regulatory, and technological pressures that shape the rapidly evolving US equities landscape.

Expert Witnessing

Building on our expertise of various aspects of market structure, we offer expert witnessing and testimony services in connection with investigations, inquiries, and proceedings, including private and governmental lawsuits, SEC, CFTC, and SRO actions, and arbitration. We also assist and advise our clients with respect to evaluating the merits and proceeding with whistleblower complaints and claims, including legal referrals.

DCM Research

DCM Research is a portal bringing together full-text documents, including proprietary research reports, and other media content provided by DCM. Topics include equities market structure, electronic trading strategies, securities regulation, market reform, and financial technology. DCM Research is currently accessible at https://decimuscapitalmarkets.com/dcm/.

DCM Zone

DCM Zone is a new framework developed by DCM in conjunction with our strategic partners to provide low-cost, rapid development capability for our clients. DCM Zone applications are deployed on an open-source platform powered by the Erlang functional programming language. Please contact us if you are interested in developing or using the DCM zone platform. DCM Zone is currently accessible at https://decimuscapitalmarkets.com/zone/.

Speaking Engagements

Haim Bodek is available for public speaking engagements, including industry conferences. His presentations cover cutting-edge topics in US equities market structure, as well as the latest high frequency trading controversies. Mr. Bodek will tailor his presentations to suit any audience, from industry insiders to laypeople. His signature dynamic speaking style always draws in attendees, contributing to your event with engaging and thought-provoking content.

Contact information:

Haim Bodek – Managing Principal
Decimus Capital Markets, LLC
203-359-2625
haim@haimbodek.com
http://haimbodek.com
https://decimuscapitalmarkets.com
Twitter: @HaimBodek